CALMING THE STORMS

Brother Richard is a Capuchin Franciscan priest-friar living and working in Ireland. His poem 'Lockdown' went viral in the early months of the coronavirus pandemic in 2020 and was translated into twenty-six languages and shared widely on traditional and social media throughout the world.

Still Points: A Guide to Living the Mindful, Meditative Way, an Irish bestseller, was published in 2022. Currently based in Dublin, Brother Richard teaches Christian meditation and mindfulness with the Sanctuary Spirituality Centre.

Find @brorichard on Instagram, Facebook and X

CALMING THE STORMS

Meditation as a Path to
Inner Peace and Happiness

Brother Richard OFM Cap

HACHETTE
BOOKS
IRELAND

First published in Ireland in 2024 by
HACHETTE BOOKS IRELAND

1

A CIP catalogue record for this title is available from the British Library.

ISBN 9781399732017

Typeset in Sabon MT Std by Palimpsest Book Production Ltd, Falkirk, Stirlingshire

Printed and bound in Great Britain by
Clays Ltd, Elcograf S.p.A.

Hachette Books Ireland policy is to use papers that are natural,
renewable and recyclable products and made from wood grown in sustainable
forests. The logging and manufacturing processes are expected to conform
to the environmental regulations of the country of origin.

Hachette Books Ireland
8 Castlecourt Centre
Castleknock
Dublin 15, Ireland

A division of Hachette UK Ltd
Carmelite House, 50 Victoria Embankment, London EC4Y 0DZ

www.hachettebooksireland.ie

Contents

Chapter 3: The Art of Awareness

Chapter 4: Meditation in the Christian Tradition

Appendix 1: Meditation, Contemplation and The Holy Eucharist

Appendix 2: Bibliography

To the Woman of Wisdom,
The Lady of the Angels,
Ancilla Domini,
Who in her total Yes
Opens the way to
Peace.

O Mary conceived without sin,
pray for us who have recourse to thee

Introduction

Most of us live, right now, in a world of storms.

Never before in history has the human being been under so much pressure from so many directions all at once. The world seems to be on fire as political systems are rocked, and new conflicts and wars are breaking out. Traditional industry and agriculture are changing, all while ecological disaster seems to threaten the very planet we walk upon as our weather patterns change, sometimes beyond recognition, and vast populations are forced into immigration just to survive.

Meanwhile the individual person is put under a constant pressure to succeed, to be perfect, to have it all, and yet to achieve balance between the professional and the personal while seeming to give 100 per cent to both at once. We are a world often obsessed with the surface and celebrity, given to a level of constant personal oversharing and fame-seeking never seen before and that we absolutely know is unhealthy, especially for the very young. Yet we cannot seem to stop. All this while being deluged by a flood of information that is available twenty-four hours a day, seven days a week. Just to stay up to date with the news is a struggle and can even affect our mental health negatively and in a lasting way if we are not careful.

We know that we are different these days, that the constant storm of both inner and outer noise is affecting our ability to focus, to relate well to others, to be patient, to know how to self-soothe and how to reach out to those in need. We know the immense numbers of those suffering from burnout, depression, anxiety, etc. often at ages so young that it beggars belief. We even speak nowadays of compassion-fatigue (a term unknown and unthinkable even a century ago) as a result of living in such a storm for so long.

I currently live and work in Dublin where the average age for first accessing the internet or having a smart phone is going down all the time. This is true for almost everywhere in the developed world. Children who have not even begun to learn who they are, or how to distinguish the false from the true, are being launched into an online world that consumes them in an almost addictive fashion and makes the previously (hopefully) safe walls of home and family and even their own inner life transparent to the world while allowing a raging storm of often highly toxic influence to take up residence in their lives. We see an externalising of self-esteem that makes it subject to the whims and opinions of others. The adults don't fare much better, trapped between evermore stressful work environments, high consumer-society expectations and the pressure to be perfect go-getters while providing a warm and nourishing familial environment all at the same time. We are worn out. How could we be anything else. Even our sleep suffers as we lie down to rest but take up the phone, or lie there worrying about the day yet to come. The storm doesn't seem to stop and our ability to take time out, to rest and restore ourselves, seems to come at a higher and higher price all of the time.

From all of the above, it should be obvious to us that the human being is not meant to live in this way, to be battered by these storms constantly. We are simply not able to process this much information and trauma, both individually and collectively, when not even two generations ago the vast majority of us lived in much smaller communities with a far quieter, more stable life, often nearer to nature and to the cycles of life and death and the seasons.

Of course, we're not entering into some kind of rosy-eyed nostalgia here. There has always been trauma; there have always been terrible things happening in families, in communities and in the world. The past is not a place where all was well. However, the difference between the past and today is that the individual then was not expected to deal with it ALL, all of the time. There was reflective space that led to the skills of focused attention naturally arising in the human being that allowed deeper questions to be asked and stories of meaning to be told, allowing the community to eventually grow in wisdom.

We know that we cannot go back, that we must live in the moment we find ourselves in and work to find a way to calm these storms that rage around us and within us, but we can look at the wisdom that the past offers us, the techniques and strategies that are part of our traditions that enable us to slow down, to live a more mindful, reflective life that allows us to choose how we engage with the world and to begin to discern what changes will help us to calm the storms that rage in our life and world today.

The traditions that invite us into a more mindful, meditative way of living teach us that there is a place at the heart of the storm where we can find a point of stillness that enables us not only to calm those storms, but also to start a new beginning every day where we can return to a centred, deep and meaningful existence.

If that longing echoes in your heart, then this book is for you.

For thousands of years the practice of meditation has been at the heart of the great wisdom traditions of the world. This practice enables us to find space in our hearts and quiet in our minds. It can bring us a depth of awareness – a way of being in the world that enables us to live the depth of our life and not just its length.

In my last book, *Still Points*, I offered a spiritual almanac to help readers journey through the four seasons of the year in a meditative way. *This* book goes deeper by providing an introduction to the practices of mindfulness and meditation, and then brings them into the Christian context so we can grow to an understanding of how, by incorporating meditation into our daily lives, we can find a way to reach calm whenever we encounter the storms of life.

Moving on from basic mindfulness practice we will then look at the four ancient paths – intention, attention, compassion and wisdom – as described by the mystical tradition of Christian monasticism, that can lead us to our still centre. These four inner directions take us on a journey that, especially when we practise them together, enable us to come to a place of stillness even while the storms rage all around us.

For almost 2,000 years, the Christian monastic tradition has taught practical ways to travel these four ancient paths, to produce in our hearts a deep awareness of the present moment as a place to encounter the Divine and to engage with all of creation, to build a deep and peaceful communion with all.

As a practitioner of this tradition, I want to share with you its richness and to introduce you to a way of living and being that will speak to your tired heart and give you hope as you look for refuge from the storms of the day.

On our journey travelling these four ancient paths,

we will encounter teachings and practices that will deepen your daily life and encourage you into a new awareness of just who you are, how you can live and 'have life, and have it in all its fullness' (John 10:10).

A Quick Word of Caution as We Begin

One of the biggest dangers in the area of meditation is to think of someone as an expert! There are no experts here – and I am certainly not presenting myself as one. You should just see me as a brother who would like to share the richness of the tradition that I try to live and practise (while often failing along the way). I hope that what I have found helpful in my own life, will be helpful in yours.

I should also say that if you are feeling a bit over-whelmed at the thought of beginning a meditative practice, please relax. You are not starting something completely new. You've probably already been mindful – the first step towards meditation – many times in your life, just without a formal structure. Every time you have had your attention engaged in the present moment – whether in a sensory experience, a creative act, a heightened moment of emotion or just being with the beauty of your surroundings – you have been mindful, and only a step or two away from meditation. So, relax, the journey ahead is one of deepening who you already are.

Well, at least you've read this far! Thank you. As you go further, this book will be a place where you will receive nourishment and enrichment to keep you going on those days when the storm rages – whether the storm is out in the world or in your own heart and mind.

To start to become aware that there are people all around us – and maybe even people you know – who place meditation and prayer at the centre of their lives is both a grace and a gift in today's world.

Simply knowing that there are others who are meditating – who are inviting God into their lives, trusting in the spirit and being in stillness and silence – is a grace that empowers our own path and makes it easier to practise ourselves.

Throughout the book I will offer a range of practices that you can use to begin and even deepen your journey into meditation. While it is wonderful to have a quiet reflective space in which to work on these exercises, they are designed to be used by anyone who can find short periods of reflective space in their day without being discommoded too much. During some of the practices you may find that it is easier to enter stillness and inner awareness by closing your eyes if you feel comfortable to do so. For those practices you may like to record the steps first on your phone so that you can play them back rather than flicking back to the text.

Finally, you will also find some poetry 'pauses' throughout the different sections of the book. These are meant as simple places to pause and to deepen our awareness of the present moment. For many of the meditative traditions, poetry and practice often go together. You may like to use the poems (maybe even read them aloud) as another kind of tool to draw yourself into a reflective space that will enable you to touch the stillness at the heart of your being.

May we lean on each other as we begin this journey together.

Brother Richard

Poetry Pause

Never Alone

Every day
there is
so much
strength
and
grace
and
beauty
to be
had
in the
knowledge
that you
are

always
being
prayed for;
that you
are never
outside
the embrace
of
Divine Love
and
Compassion;
But are
held there
by those
often
hidden souls
who dedicate
their lives
to
meditation
and prayer . . .
Trust me;
you are
never
alone . . .

Chapter 1

Mindfulness - The First Step towards Meditation

The practice of mindfulness is everywhere today! However, what is often missed nowadays is that, traditionally, the practice of mindfulness was simply the first step towards deeper meditative practice. In this chapter we will begin our journey into meditation by looking at what mindfulness is, the necessity of developing the quality of mindful attention and then how it leads us towards deeper forms of practice.

When I was a novice (a monk in training) – not too many years ago but getting longer as the beard turns white – our teacher, the Novice Master, told us that we were expected, at all times, to have a 'recollected mind and a mortified disposition'. Sadly, I'm still working on the second one, but I have learned that, just like most of the great religions in the world, the call to have a 'recollected mind' has always been at the heart of the Christian meditative tradition.

The basis of this tradition is that your mind – your way of relating with the world – is very often distracted, broken up and divided, and that there is healing to be found in collecting these broken pieces and bringing them together into a quiet way of being. And in that stillness, you become aware of the depth of your own being and even of the presence of God.

This is what Christians have been doing – or at least trying to do – since the foundation of their faith. One of the practice tools that enables us to take the path of inner attention is mindfulness, which makes it a core practice when learning to meditate.

Mindfulness

Ask yourself what picture comes to mind when you hear the word 'mindfulness'.

Create that picture in your mind right now before you read any further . . .

Got it?

Let's check in and see what you came up with.

For most people in Western society, the images that emerge tend to be of Buddhist monks, zen landscapes and yoga classes – the result of our Instagram-informed imaginations perhaps.

But mindfulness as a beginning point on the path

of meditation is part of every great world religion. There are forms of it found in Hinduism, Buddhism, Taoism, Islam and, often to people's surprise, in Judaism and Christianity too.

Of course, today, mindfulness is often practised in a non-religious way too. As Professor Mark Williams of Oxford University (where they have been studying mindfulness and its effects for nearly twenty years) defines it, mindfulness is simply a human quality of awareness, a way of 'paying attention on purpose, in the present moment, with compassion and open-hearted curiosity'.

If we focus on the present moment, if we really listen and give it our attention, then we are being mindful.

Modern Mindfulness

While people have always practised mindfulness, the current popularity of mindfulness began with Dr Jon Kabat-Zinn of Boston University. He is a psychologist and has worked with people who have various psychological problems, particularly those who experience recurring depression.

He noted that we can often obsess over the past or worry about the future, and this is not healthy. Not being in the present can generate anxiety and can complicate depression; it may negatively affect our mental and social well-being. This is why the practice of mindfulness has become such a popular skill in the fields of mental health and education.

Kabat-Zinn undertook a retreat with the Zen Buddhist monk Thich Nhat Hanh and came to realise that a lot of the exercises that the monk was offering about being aware of the present moment would be hugely beneficial to people who were suffering from anxiety and depression. Out of this realisation, he created what was called the Mindfulness Based Stress Reduction (MBSR) course.

Today, this course is taught all over the world, and there is ample evidence to show that it can help people who experience anxiety, periods of extended stress or depression. You can read his fascinating book *Full Catastrophe Living* if you would like to know more.

Kabat-Zinn and others have done a lot of work to identify the different applications of mindfulness in health care, and we now have mindfulness-based cognitive therapy (MBCT) for people who are struggling with changing their patterns of behaviour.

There are other scientists such as Daniel Siegal who have even worked on the neurobiology of mindfulness and have looked at questions like: How does mindfulness affect our brains? What does it do within our brains and bodies?

Professor Richard Davidson, from the wonderfully named Center for Investigating Healthy Minds at the University of Madison and Wisconsin, has done extraordinary work in this whole area. He has shown that the neuroplasticity of the brain – the ability of the brain to reprogramme itself, to grow and find new ways of doing things – is particularly stimulated through mindful awareness.

The modern revolution in mindfulness from a scientific perspective supports the basic teaching that all religions have, to some extent, taught us down the ages. Namely, that being still, silent and focused is necessary to develop a spiritual life, and we can use that stillness to build a life that centres around meditation.

To put it even more simply, mindfulness can help us to be fully human and present.

Of course, there are essential differences between various traditions and religions, both in method and goals. The ultimate goal of meditation in the Christian tradition is to arrive at an awareness of the presence of God. We practise becoming still so that we may know and be supported by God (Psalm 46) and, through our knowing Him, we find that He already knows us. The Christian belief is that God knows us and loves us – that we have been loved into being, that love is holding us and that love is calling us to be one with God for eternity.

But we find ourselves distracted from this path of awareness. Our mind is scattered – as the old Catechism would say, the 'intellect is darkened'. When we really look within ourselves and examine those distractions in detail, we find that we do not perceive reality as it is, but experience it through a veil of self-centredness and external conditioning.

You must practise mindfulness – this stillness and attentiveness – to quieten your mind, heart and spirit when you have become overwhelmed by the world around you.

As I mentioned in the introduction, we all have these moments of mindfulness already. However, because of our distracted state, we often experience them only in response to the highest and the lowest moments of our lives.

In the Christian tradition mindfulness is used to help us be in a state that persists in between the highs and lows of life. This gives us a calm centre from which we can address all that is going on both within and without ourselves.

This is why the practice of mindfulness has become such a popular skill in the fields of mental health and education, even in its most basic relaxation forms. However, in the Christian tradition, we believe that mindfulness will take us into the regions of the soul and the heart, where we can encounter the presence of God.

A wonderful study of a group of Catholic nuns and the place meditation and mindfulness played in their lives was published in 2011 by Dr David Snowden, under the title *Aging with Grace*, which illustrates this point further. The sisters involved allowed a group of behavioural scientists and neurobiologists to study them as they grew older.

One wonderful finding was that many of the sisters were much clearer in their cognitive faculties and much more empathetic and compassionate than would be expected from people of a similar chronological age. At first, the scientists couldn't work out why this would be so. They began to send young doctors and nurses in to sit and talk to them regularly. From these conversations, it was concluded that the sisters engaged in three simple practices that most older people give up, don't practise or have had taken from them by the circumstances of their old age. And that these three practices kept the nuns young.

The first practice was community. The nuns continued to live in a caring, compassionate community right into their old age.

The second was mindful prayer. The nuns sat regularly in a disciplined way in simple stillness and silence, and this gave their brains the opportunity to reprogramme and even heal.

The third practice was that, for as long as they could, the sisters engaged in work that was meaning-centred — work that was carried out in a fully attentive way, rather than just for a wage.

Isn't that interesting? Mindfulness can have a wonderful effect on our physical being.

Let's take a brief look at what happens when we begin to pay attention mindfully.

The Mindful Brain

Human beings tend to live in patterned behaviours. We perform a behaviour and, if it works, we do it again and again and again, until we don't have to think about how to do it anymore.

Think of a simple action, like brushing your teeth, or even a very complicated one, like driving. At the start, someone had to teach you these skills. We become better at them each time we practise them and, over time, they become second nature to us. So much so that we can be conscious of other things while we are doing them. This, of course, is very useful for survival. After a while these skills consciously learned originally can become unconscious patterns that we repeat mindlessly, not even asking if they are useful to us anymore.

The real problem occurs when this patterning becomes the main way we operate in life.

Mindfulness is a skill that enables us to reflect on our patterns of behaviour and to begin to recognise which patterns are positive and useful, and which are negative and less useful.

An image that may be useful here is to see your mind as a labyrinth – an image that was often used in the medieval times. A labyrinth is not a maze – you do not get lost in a labyrinth – you simply go deeper within as the path of the labyrinth forces you to slow down and, eventually, you come to a centre point that gives you the possibility of a more intense and aware overview of your route.

In medieval times, a labyrinth was used as a form of inner journeying. It was considered so sacred a practice that great labyrinths were built, often found in or near the cathedrals. Walking the labyrinth was thought to have the same spiritual value as pilgrimages to holy places. In walking them, you would find that you would slow down, have time to reflect on your life – and so you are changed.

Unfortunately, today, most of us are not walking the labyrinthian way. In our too-fast and distracted lives, we simply repeat circles of behaviour, over and over again, often with the same results. These behaviours may have worked for us in the past, they may even have been necessary in the past, but now we seem to be subject to them rather than the other way around.

You see, if you walk a circle of behaviour often enough, you will eventually dig a trench from which there is simply no escape. After a while, you may even forget that there ever was any landscape outside the trench at all.

You will need help or an intervention to be raised up and brought back to the place where you had choice and, even then, and with the best will in the world, you may choose the trench again, even without necessarily wanting to.

The world shrinks for us when we repeat patterns

that are not useful anymore and our choices seem to shrink with it.

At one stage, I was living in a midlands town in Ireland that had a facility for those suffering from mental-health problems. Many of those who lived there were long-term residents – confined at a time when those with mental-health issues were placed behind high walls and forgotten.

Thankfully, by the time I was living nearby, things had changed. The walls had come down – literally and figuratively – a few years earlier and the residents were encouraged to take their rightful place in society while still receiving the support they needed from the staff.

I would often take a shortcut through the facility's immaculately landscaped grounds and, sometimes, would stop to chat with the residents. There were those, however, for whom the removal of physical walls had meant very little. They would go for their walk each day and trace the route of where the walls used to be, turning at right angles where the corners had been – even though a couple more steps would have taken them out and into the town. This was the route they had walked every day for years – for some for twenty or thirty years. Even though the physical walls had come down, the walls still existed in their minds.

This rather extreme example shows how strong our patterning instinct is and how, with enough repetition, we can find ourselves walking in a mental trench or being locked behind invisible walls without being aware that this is what is happening.

At the very least, mindfulness invites you to look at how you can change and grow. It asks how you can change for the better, how you can live more deeply and be aware of the moment, just for that moment.

Mindfulness in a Christian practice goes deeper, of course. We practise mindfulness to live the duty of the moment. If we live the duty of the moment, we are sowing seeds of a deeper, more attentive relationship with Divine Love.

A simple way of enabling the practice of mindfulness to make a difference to the patterns in our lives is to practise 'checking in' mindfully. This helps us into a deeper experience of daily life. Let's try this now.

Practice: The Mindful Check-In

This practice may be done anywhere and at any time. It can be really helpful as a way of discovering those times when we are operating out of a patterning mindset. At first, until you get used to doing it regularly, you may want to come to a moment of bodily stillness that will help you be with each question as it is considered.

Find a comfortable seat in a quiet space, place your feet flat on the floor and keep your back comfortably straight, take a moment to settle yourself and simply pause.

Then ask yourself the following questions:

- What am I feeling right now?

- What am I thinking right now?

- What am I noticing around me?

- What is my breath doing?

- What do I need to do to take care of this moment with compassion and peace?

Once you have gently cycled through the questions and feel like you have answered them, then take a nice deep breath in and out and re-enter the activity of the day.

If we practise this routine regularly then, over time, we will find that even though we are continuing to do what we already do, we are now doing it with gentle awareness, and this will help us change our patterns.

Of course, as well as just checking in, we also want to put some time aside for deeper moments of practice.

When we begin to practise, and even pray, in a mindful way, we discover that the day can become more spacious. This is because we are now living in a more aware way that enables us to begin to hold on to patterns that are still useful and helpful (like driving, showering, eating, exercising etc.) while letting go of patterns that perhaps served us once but no longer are as useful as they were at one time. For example, a person who as a child is bullied will often learn to live in a hypervigilant way. As a child this is a useful pattern that enables the child to protect themselves and stay safe. However, as they leave the bullying environment behind and transition into adulthood, such a pattern can have negative effects on the way they relate to others and even to themselves, causing them to continue to live at a hypervigilant and stressed level when such a pattern no longer serves them. Without mindful awareness, such negative patterns can continue to hold sway over our behaviour without us realising where they came from or even why they are there.

I remember once co-teaching a course on mindfulness and education for teachers. One of the practices we brought to the teachers who were attending the course was known as 'the mindful piece of chocolate'. In that exercise the teachers were shown how to introduce the practice of mindful eating to children by inviting them to slow down to enjoy with the full awareness of their senses just one square of chocolate. At the end of bringing one group of teachers through the practice, one woman seemed a little upset. On inquiring as to why, she told us that we had 'taken away chocolate from her life'. We were surprised! Had we not just given her some? On diving a little deeper in reflection with her, we discovered that the act of slowing down to mindfully eat the chocolate had revealed to her that she did not actually like chocolate! This came as a huge surprise, considering it had been her practice to take a cup of coffee and a bar of milk chocolate every day as her 'me time' after school. Now, having slowed down and brought mindful awareness to the act of eating, she realised that her body did not like the taste of chocolate. As we inquired a little further, she realised that she had been using chocolate as an emotional reward for good behaviour just as her mother had done with her many years ago. A pattern had been formed, it had become unconscious and a feeling of being 'good' was generated by the act of eating the chocolate even though her adult body actually didn't like the taste. Afterwards she decided that the important thing to carry forward was the practice of taking a few moments of peace with her coffee after school. The chocolate wasn't needed anymore. There was now a space to choose something new.

So there is more room when we are not consumed by our negative patterns of behaviour, when we live the day without the day living us, as it were.

The problems come when we feel stress or anxiety and, in those moments, we are likely to give up our check-ins – and our practice – in order to sort out the things immediately in front of us, and this is when we will often fall back into our patterns.

When we understand the patterning that is part of all of our lives, we can begin to ask: Do I want to change some of these patterns and become a better version of who I am? Or am I just going around again and again without either resolution or significant change?

Mindfulness invites us to reflect on how we *can* change. How we can grow and how we can deepen our experience of who we are by recognising our patterns and by beginning to discern how to hold on to the good patterns – the positive and useful ones – and let go of the negative ones.

It sounds easy, doesn't it? But there's a problem . . .

The Stress Funnel

Psychologists have long spoken of the stress funnel – that feeling of life becoming narrower and tighter when we jettison the practices that support our spiritual and mental well-being and return to our negative patterns in order to get things done.

We soon find that all we can focus on is the problem in front of us that we have been trying to solve or escape from. The great spiritual master St Francis de Sales considered half an hour of meditation a day as essential, except when we find ourselves anxious or too busy, in which case an hour is essential!

Practice: Deepening the Check-In

Find a comfortable seat in a quiet space, place your feet flat on the floor and keep your back comfortably straight, take a moment to settle yourself and simply pause.

A good practice, then, to add to our mindful check-in, as described on page 21, is to ask yourself the following questions:

- Is your life widening or narrowing?

- Is your life shallower or deeper at present?

- Where are the pressures to make your life narrower or shallower coming from?

- What would widening or deepening your life look like?

- Is there anything you need to let go of or take on that could help you to widen or deepen your life. (Feel free to dream as big, to be as aspirational and creative as you wish in this answer.)

- What could you do, in this moment, to restore some width and depth to your life?

The Lazy Brain

One of the things that gets in the way of change, of our ability to move on from negative patterns to a more mindful, dynamic way of life, is that we also have a lazy brain.

All of us – every human being – is fundamentally lazy. We may want to change – at least we want to begin to change – but our resolve is easily shaken by the call of the familiar and our well-trodden patterns.

'I will begin tomorrow!' we say. But then we think a little and realise that we can't begin tomorrow because tomorrow is a Sunday. And who begins things on a Sunday? 'So, I will begin on Monday,' we tell ourselves. 'I'll definitely start on Monday. Monday is a good day to begin!'

And then Monday comes and, you know, it is a Monday – so we sit over our cup of coffee and we look out the window and we say, 'You know, maybe Tuesday will be better,' and so on.

This is where living mindfully will help us. We realise that it is not about New Year's resolutions or beginning tomorrow: it's about simply asking yourself what you can do now, in this moment. How can you live more deeply, more compassionately and with greater curiosity in an open-hearted way right now, in this moment?

The thing to remember is that, if you miss this moment, there is another moment just about to come along.

As we develop mindful awareness, we will find that it tends to first call in on the body, then on the mind and only then on the soul. By minding our bodies and minds, and developing a mindful approach, we are more easily able to look into our hearts, the very essence of who we are.

In the Christian tradition our mindful awareness asks us to consider what is the cry of the soul in the present moment? It is always calling for and seeking the presence of God. This is true no matter what we are doing – even if we are only drinking a cup of coffee, we can do it mindfully and with intention, so that it becomes not just a mindful action but also a prayer.

The aim is to recognise what we do every day and then to do these things mindfully.

In the monastic tradition, we try and hold the conscious awareness that the ultimate origin of all that is good is God. Even our morning cup of coffee that we experience mindfully ultimately comes from God.

We are being held by Divine Love, so the moment I experience mindfully is always, at its heart, a moment of love, reflecting on love and coming from love.

We find it hard to accept that we can make 'hallow' – make holy with attention – even the most ordinary and earthly of our activities because we have been brought up to see a dichotomy between the spiritual and the earthly.

I remember being at a retreat where, after a lecture about meditative topics with a monk, a middle-aged man in a three-piece suit objected that, while all of these practices were wonderful for monks and nuns, he was far too busy to take on the practice of mindfulness.

The monk simply smiled and asked if he could put one query to him. When the man agreed, he was asked gently, 'Tell me, do you use the bathroom during the day?'

When the man said that of course he did, the monk said, 'Begin there, just do all that you do in there mindfully and with attention.'

While this may seem a little humorous, there is a great truth at its heart: that even the most basic bodily functions may be seen as signals to call us to attentive moments of mindful awareness.

Grace is not just a practice for before and after the meal; it is a practice of blessing the entire experience of the meal. With this as our fundamental attitude, even the bathroom – as many a stressed-out parent or employee will tell you – can be a sanctuary for a moment or two of recalibration in a busy home or workplace.

Another example of the nature of attending mindfully to the simple needs of the body may be gleaned from the Monastery of St Gall, one of the great monastic houses of the early Middle Ages that sent missionaries and scholars across Europe.

Some years ago, the floor plan of the monastery was discovered hidden away in the bindings of one of the volumes in the library. Historians studied it to learn about the way in which a medieval monastery was organised, and they found that there was only one block listed as the 'Necessarium' – which is necessary.

It wasn't the chapel or the library. It was, of course, the bathrooms. Once again, a little reminder that we do not mount to deep meditation without attending to the basic needs of the body first, or the needs of the body will continually make themselves known and disrupt our practice.

Without meeting those needs – at least until we have learned deep mindfulness – the mind will become obsessed with what is missing and we will make little progress. We must begin with what is natural and ordinary, sanctify it with deliberate awareness.

In our Christian understanding, everything is fundamentally good in its origin and its essence. This means that everything that the Lord provides for us – for our bodies, minds and hearts – can be used as a way of being present and with Him even in our very busy life and home.

We practise being mindful of small things first, of the smell of the coffee; we try to be fully present to it, to take a moment of stillness. We are not afraid of recognising that those little beans are gifts to us. As a Capuchin, I'm very fond of stressing the coffee thing as the cappuccino is named after us!

Let's begin with a simple presence exercise that will help us to enter into the present moment a little more deeply.

Practice: A Presence Exercise

This is an exercise that allows you to come into deeper awareness of yourself as you exist in the present moment. While it can be done anywhere you will not be disturbed, at the start and until you are used to the practice it is better to do it regularly in a quiet, comfortable space where you can sit in a relaxed but aware manner. You may like to record the instruction to listen to it with eyes closed, or gaze softened and lowered.

Find a comfortable seat in a quiet space, place your feet flat on the floor and with your back comfortably straight, take a moment to settle yourself and simply pause.

Set a three-minute timer on your phone or watch.

Once you have settled in, gently become aware of your breath as you breathe in and out.

Do not change the rhythm of the breath in anyway – just notice it as it flows in and out at its own pace.

Can you feel the coolness of the breath as it enters the body through the mouth or nose?

Can you feel the warmth of the breath as it leaves the body?

The breath is an anchor to the present moment.

We are always breathing in the present moment.

No matter what else we are doing, if we are alive, we are breathing.

Bring your attention to the sensations and movement in your abdomen, as you breathe in and out.

You may find it helpful to place a hand on your abdomen to support you.

If you find your mind wanders at any time, just notice where it has gone, and gently but firmly guide your attention back to your abdomen and your next breath.

When the alarm signals you are to finish, check in with yourself and, perhaps, offer a short prayer or good wish of gratitude for this gentle mindful moment.

Poetry Pause

Minding the Moment

You have only
to breathe. . .
That's all.
Breathe in
and out.
The next moment
will follow.
As will the next day.
You are not
responsible
for the running
of the
universe.
(Thank God.)
Remember this,

as you breathe
in and
out.
All that was
can be left behind.
It was only as good
as the wisdom it gave.
All that is yet to be
is unknown.
It will come,
it will be,
it will pass,
it will leave wisdom
(if you allow it to),
but for now
it is not here yet.
All that is needed
now,
absolutely needed
now,
is this
breath,
in
and
out.
To be,
breathe.
To act nourishingly,
breathe gently.

To pray,
breathe with awareness.
But above all,
just
breathe.
Build your
life
from
the breath
up.
Life can
only
be lived
one
sacred breath
at a time.
Then,
as you dwell
in the
awareness
of just
this
breath,
slowly,
gently,
you will find
that Love
is breathing
you into

being.
All you have
to do,
to begin,
now,
this moment,
is
breathe.

Chapter 2

The Benefits of Mindfulness

When you engage in mindfulness regularly and with discipline, you will start to notice various benefits from your efforts.

The first thing you will notice is an increase in the quality of awareness.

Awareness

What do we mean by awareness? When we are more aware, we are more present to our external environment and to what's going on within us.

This can be a wonderfully beneficial thing, as it enables us to be less instantly reactive than we may have been before. Awareness takes away reactivity and helps us to live in the present moment as a reflective experience.

This means that our present reality is seen more deeply and encountered by our reflective capacity, rather than snap judgements. When practised regularly, awareness enables us to move our base state of being from one that goes through life like a pinball game, reacting to the 'other' – stimuli that is external to us and often beyond our control – to one where we have a more reflective strategy. Where we can experience life more as a game of chess, where we can have a strategy to reach our goals, but also be flexible to respond to stimuli, but only after considered reflection.

Practice: Awareness Exercises

1. Find a comfortable seat in a quiet space, place your feet flat on the floor and your back comfortably straight, take a moment to settle yourself and simply pause. Take a moment to sit gently with your hands resting in your lap. Turn up your palms.

   Gently rest your gaze on your hands; take time to notice them – to really notice them. Begin to notice all the sensations you can feel in your hands. Notice the difference in sensation between the backs of your hands and the palms. Look out for any sensation in the fingers or between the fingers. Notice any difference in sensation between the left hand and the right hand. Gently investigate these sensations without judgement.

Notice any subtle movements in your hands, any warmth or coolness, any heaviness or lightness. Be thankful for the gift of your hands.

2. When you are out walking begin to notice how you walk. Take a few moments to really feel the movement of your legs, the roll of your soles against the pavement. Feel the pressure on your toes and on your heels.

Notice what the rest of your body is doing as you walk. How are your hips or your shoulders moving? What about your arms and hands or your neck and head? Do not change your normal gait, but just notice what it is to walk or to move in any way. Try and aim to notice sensations that you are not ordinarily aware of.

3. The next time you are drinking a cup of tea or coffee really notice the sensations that you experience. Be present to the flavour of the drink, ask yourself when was the last time you truly tasted this drink. Allow all of your senses to be present. Feel the warmth of the mug in your hands. Become aware of the steam as it dissolves in the air. Notice all the sensations of drinking from the moment the liquid touches

your lips to the moment that the liquid vanishes after you swallow it.

The Quality of Liminality

The second quality that is often seen to arise from our practice of mindfulness is liminality. Now what we mean by this is the deliberately chosen and practised ability to be content not being at the centre of things. To know that it's okay to be at the edge – and that the edge is often a good place to develop a deeper quality of awareness. The edge bestows perspective and the space to reflect and make choices that are not based on unconscious patterns and the expectations of others.

After all, we live in a very egocentric world that tells us we have to be interesting and entertaining twenty-four-seven.

Think of the worst excesses of social media and reality television. They are telling us that we must be at the very centre of things all the time, that everybody should be looking at us and that we should compare ourselves and our levels of fame – or even centrality to the ongoing narrative of society – to everyone else.

This is an exhausting and often morally empty way to live.

Liminality enables us to begin to live from the depth of our life, rather than the length of it. In this understanding, when we are living from the length of life we are subject to external stimuli that cause reactions without any kind of reflective choice making. This is the classic dopamine-addiction lifestyle where we seek constant affirmation and, if necessary, alter who we are in order to receive it. Living the quality of liminality brings us instead into the depth of our lives by choosing the edge spaces of life; we make space for reflection that enables wisdom to grow. We are no longer subject to the opinions and demands of others but begin to learn who we are and organise our lives around a new sense of inner identity. The quality of liminality, arising as it does from mindful practice, challenges many of the assumptions that we too-often accept from the predominant twenty-first-century Western culture. It enables us to value our own individual experiences, without getting lost in an exalted sense of individualism, and it enables a mutuality to build by honouring the different gifts of those around us, which we see more clearly from our liminal position, while developing the ability to offer our own gifts to the collective whole in compassionate service.

Moving towards the edge enables us to gain a real sense of perspective, even to become more aware of our needs and the needs of those around us, rather than living in a small echo-chamber of our own ideas, egoic (self-centred) projections and false judgements. It is a path of wisdom honoured and respected by most of the great religious traditions of humanity, as it produces a deep and healthy humility.

Thus, we begin to be aware of the depth dimension to our lives. We begin to be aware that the transcendent dimensions of life are all around us, and within us too. Heaven is everywhere and every bush, every tree, every flower is afire with the glory of God – but you can't see it unless you slow down and breathe and are present to it. As G.K. Chesterton wrote in *The Defendant*: 'Most probably we are in Eden still. It is only our eyes that have changed.'

Practice: Liminality Exercises

1. Go to a busy café by yourself. Sit down with your coffee or cup of tea; take a few moments to settle comfortably into your chair. Then slowly begin to notice all the interactions around you.

   Let your circle of awareness grow outwards from yourself to the tables next to you and then, finally, to the edges of the room. Allow yourself to receive a sensory experience of the totality of the room.

   At first this may seem to be chaotic but, after a while, you will notice your attention being drawn to encounters with meaning arising from your sensory experience. Receive these without judgement and without creating any narrative. For example, if you hear a little of a conversation from a table next to you, do not begin to imagine you know how or why that conversation has arisen: simply acknowledge it, be present to it.

From time to time, draw your attention back to yourself and notice any reactions you have, especially any attempts to make judgements or suppositions about those around you. Simply recall yourself again and again to the action of being present.

2. Try to cultivate the habit of standing back within yourself during conversations to ask yourself if you are truly listening to the other person or are you waiting to speak. Ask yourself what you are noticing about the other person. What level of emotion are they speaking with? What level of commitment to their topic do they have? Notice any snap judgements you have made about them based on what they are saying or how they are communicating. Try to listen with your whole being and be attentive through all of your senses.

3. Before going to bed at night take a few moments to look back over your day and recognise those times when you could have practised liminality by listening deeply. Check your own assumptions or judgements. Did you insert yourself

into conversations or debates simply for the egoic spark within you?

Mark these without any emotion and simply resolve to learn from them going forward. Then let them go.

Silence

Together, awareness and liminality can also produce the fruit of inner silence. This is not an empty, scary silence but a warm and wise place of evolving wisdom.

This quality of silence moves you past the constant chatter of your distracted mind and into a place of peace. You begin to discover that it is really rather wonderful to be silent, even sometimes within a conversation. This is the silence that occurs when you are really listening to the other person. It is not the silence of desperately hoping they will shut up so we can speak, nor is it the cold silence of disregard.

This silence enables real reflection and consideration and the slow distillation of wisdom from our experience. It welcomes the other and what they have to say as a possible source of truth and wisdom – it always considers them from this fundamentally optimistic place.

Practice: Silence Exercises

1. Find a comfortable seat in a quiet space, place your feet flat on the floor and your back comfortably straight, take a moment to settle yourself and simply pause. Take a silence audit of your day. Remember the moments when you could have cultivated silence more readily. Notice how often an otherwise silent space was filled by the radio, podcasts, TV, your phone, music or other media.

   Try to begin your day with silence – even if only for a few moments. Throughout the day, choose a moment of silence every hour or two to simply be with yourself and check in with yourself (you could do the check-in exercises mentioned earlier). This will help you to begin to see silence as necessary and as beneficial to your well-being.

2. When you are out and about in nature – whether in your garden, walking in the park, or simply journeying between work and home – take some time to notice the natural sounds around you and allow yourself to become present to those sounds.

   At the start, it may be useful to name them as they make themselves known to your awareness. Then begin to notice the silence from which they arise and which exists around and between them.

3. Take a few moments simply to sit comfortably and rest in the silence around you. If you are not used to silence, this may seem uncomfortable and even a little scary at first, as your mind will jump to distractions. But if you persevere, you will find that simply sitting in silence while observing without judgement whatever arises in your mind or body leads to a gentle state of relaxed awareness.

This is in fact the beginning of the path to deeper meditation. At the start, try for three minutes, twice a day.

Compassion

Another beneficial fruit that we hope to see rising from the practice of mindfulness is compassion. In the West today, we tend to think of compassion as simply being kind or reaching out to help another person. While this is very important, it is a lesser understanding of what compassion is.

In its essence, compassion means 'being with' or 'being present to' the person who is suffering (*cum passio* means 'with suffering' in Latin). Sometimes, all we can do for the person suffering – or even for ourselves when we are the ones suffering – is to choose to be present, to be aware and to witness in a way that does not impose false hopes or solutions but will invite a deep courage and loving presence.

Working with the homeless, as many of my fellow friars have done over the years, is to become very aware of the power of this compassionate gaze that is not in any way patronising but is deeply human and loving.

When asked what they need most, many of those going through homelessness answer that when the basic biological needs of food and shelter have been met, they want to be seen. To be seen is important because they sit on the street and people choose not to see them and even those who give something often don't look at them and don't spend time with them.

Now, we're all guilty of this at times, me included. We are busy. We need to move on, to get past the obstacle or the distraction. But wouldn't it be wonderful if we gave people the gift of compassionate presence? This is actually compassion in action – attending to the person that this moment has presented to you and listening deeply to their need. Even if we can't alleviate that need there and then, to have at least listened well is a great act of compassion.

I remember hearing on one occasion about a group of pre-school children who were asked 'What is a grandmother?' The answer they gave was that a grandmother is someone 'who has time for me'. Isn't that a wonderful definition? Somebody who has time to be with you and to listen to your need because mum and dad or others are so busy with life.

Compassion is born of listening in the present moment when we share the two most important resources we have – time and attention.

Practice: Compassion Exercises

1. Take a few moments to sit or stand in front of a mirror. Notice how quickly your mind jumps to judgement or to a negative narrative. Gently, move your mind back to the present moment by gazing into your own eyes. Ask yourself: When was the last time I looked on myself without judgement?

   Rest a few moments in the awareness of how long it has been. Then, let your gaze widen to take in the features of your face, and more of your body if the mirror is big enough. Remind yourself that all of your countless ancestors have contributed to the building of your body and that it is wonderfully made.

   You may like to stop with this thought or, if you feel able, you can proceed to a moment of inner gratitude for the gift of your body.

2. As you go through the day, nurture the inner resolution as much as you can so those you encounter along the way will find compassion in you.

   As you encounter a friend or stranger, colleague or family member, notice your first reaction to them and whether or not you need to practise the awareness of their need for compassion in that moment. Notice how this changes the encounters you have throughout the day.

3. Take some moments to enter into comfortable stillness with your feet grounded on the floor and your hands resting on your lap. Ask yourself who is in your circle of compassion and then begin to picture them. Ask yourself who has shown you compassion in your life and picture them. Dwell for a few moments in gratitude for both groups.

   Then, ask yourself what you have learned about being compassionate from both of these groups. Finally, resolve to bring these elements of compassion to everyone you encounter.

Kindness

The final quality or fruit arising from the practice of mindfulness we can look at here is genuine kindness.

In Ancient Greece, this type of kindness was often

referred to as *metis*. It includes a kindness towards the self. We are invited to be kind towards ourselves because, very often, the worst judge you will ever face is yourself because you're trying to live up to expectations that you have absorbed unknowingly from others around you, or even from the media and society at large.

These expectations are often impossible to fulfil. Kindness reminds us that we are human beings and that means we are fallible. Being human means that we can often be broken. It means that we are often distracted, often lost in egoic selfishness and even susceptible to what the Christian tradition calls sin and other traditions call negative deeds or the generation of evil thoughts or actions.

All of these bits and pieces – the failing, the falling, the brokenness, the sin – all of that is not the essence of who you are.

Our mindful meditative practice shows us that when we live from the essence of who we are then not only do those things begin to transform and change, but we also become much kinder towards ourselves, more gentle and understanding. This in turn leads to a greater kindness to others as we learn that other people are also struggling in this way.

It takes patience to grow in kindness towards yourself while not losing discipline. Patience every single day, beginning again each day – as one of the monastic fathers said, 'I must keep beginning until I end.'

Practice: Kindness Exercises

1. Find a comfortable seat in a quiet space, place your feet flat on the floor and with your back comfortably straight, take a moment to settle yourself and simply pause. Take a few moments to come to dwell in awareness. You may like to begin with the earlier presence exercise as a way of coming to stillness. When you feel you have settled into the awareness that comes from being present to the normal ebb and flow of the breath within you, move on to take three cycles of breath in and out, this time holding your breath for a moment longer than usual before releasing it and breathing out. Let your out-breath also be slightly longer than usual. Then return to your normal rhythm of breath and notice any different sensations in the body. Recognise the gift you have given yourself in this moment by taking time to dwell in awareness of the breath. (As you get used to this way of breathing you can move into breathing like this for about three minutes, which can really deepen our relaxation response.)

2. Ask yourself how you can be more kind to your own being in a way that will lead to a deeper experience of life. Take some time to consider this. Begin by checking in with your bodily

needs and then slowly move your awareness to your emotional needs and your relational needs, such as how you would like to be treated by those around you.

3. Every morning take a moment to resolve to perform at least one act of random kindness to a stranger during the day. As far as possible, do these anonymously. In the evening, take some time to notice how often you have managed to do this and how it makes you feel. If you were unable to achieve such deeds do not 'stew' over them but simply practise beginning again the following day.

4. Try to resolve each day to be aware, so that when empathy or compassion are triggered by a real-life encounter or something in the media, you pause long enough to ask how you can be kind in that situation in word or deed. As time goes on, also notice when negative feelings or judgements are triggered and ask the same question – how can I be kind in this situation in word or deed?

Poetry Pause

The Call of Dawn

Outside my
window
the world is
being created
anew, again.
Dawn resolves
all into form
once more,
darkness slowly
rolling back
like mist before
the gentle touch
of light.
And even before the
sun arrives
the feathered heralds
are calling all
to attend.
For a moment,
Eden breathes
across the land,
again,
and I am woken
to watch.
What a blessing

to be here,
at the hinge
of the day,
unworthy,
but called
to witness
the movement
from night to day,
the moment
of bright blessing
that shows Divine faith
in us, again.
That offers in response
to our
sleepy selves
always a
new beginning.
That yearns
for us to stand
attending
to the moment,
to the grace
of a today
that will never
come again,
to a new dawn,
to a new blessing
of beginning.

Chapter 3

The Art of Awareness

Christians have been teaching mindfulness since the very beginning of the monastic tradition. It is just a new word for an old set of skills that were used to ready the mind and heart for deeper forms of meditation.

In the past, we would have referred to mindfulness as 'contemplative awareness' or 'inner watchfulness'. The distinctive difference of Christian mindfulness is that being mindful through Christian practices is centred on a particular goal – to become more aware of the presence of God, 'The One in whom we live and move and have our being' (cf. Acts 17:28).

Mindfulness in the Scriptures

In the Old Testament, there is a word for mindfulness that is used again and again – *kavanah*. Simply put, *kavanah* means having your heart or mind focused on God in the midst of your day-to-day life, but especially in moments of prayer or spiritual activity.

Often in their writings, the prophets warned that 'These people honour me with their lips, but their hearts are far from me' (Is 29:13).

In other words, if when people were praying, they were not fully focused on their words, and on the intention behind them – they were not being present to God with their hearts, with the fullness of their awareness.

When Jesus comes into the world He is calling the people to a conversion of heart that will see us recentred on the revelation of the presence of God – of Divine Love – in their lives and in the world around them.

Jesus teaches us that 'the kingdom of God is within you' (LK 17:21). In this, He means that we may come to know the presence of God in the depths of our own being, a place often referred to in scripture as the 'heart'.

When we speak of the heart in this way, we are not, of course, speaking of the physical organ or the popular romanticised idea of the 'Valentine' heart as a place of emotion and feeling: we mean the centre of our entire being. This is the place that is distinctly me. It is the place within myself where I can find God.

Again and again, throughout the scriptures, people are called to an awareness of the presence of God within their hearts. He abides with them, moment by moment, and is closer to them than their own breath.

The cultivation of this awareness – this *kavanah* – was seen by the early Christians and especially by the first monastics, as the prerequisite of all prayer, meditation and spiritual practice. Indeed, it was considered essential to live a fully human life. Without *kavanah*, without mindfulness, prayer was empty – it was just ritualism. It is the conversion of the heart that brings it to rest in the presence of God.

The practice of *kavanah* bestowed what we call the 'quality of attending', of being mindful of God in all the moments and activities of our lives. In many respects, this was the whole purpose of the old law: to enable people to live in a covenanted relationship with God that would, through the law's practices and observances, lead to an experiential awareness of the presence of God.

Jesus on Prayer and Meditation

As we move into the Christian understanding of meditation, we must begin by going to the gospels and asking what Christ taught us about meditation and prayer.

Firstly, we may look at the example of His own being. He attends the liturgies of the synagogue and the temple. He keeps the Passover and the other Jewish feasts, and He withdraws into solitude and silence for whole nights of communion with the Father, especially before major events and decisions.

In showing us how to pray, He gives us two great teachings – the first is the 'Our Father', which is given to us as the pattern of all prayer, and there Jesus situates prayer as the path of transformational communion with God. With the giving of the Our Father we receive a map that will guide us, initiate us into a new way of relating to God. He is our 'Abba' our beloved father in the fullest and most nurturing understanding of this name. The prayer reveals our communitarian meditative path (He is 'Our' father, we relate to Him as community first); it keeps us mindful of Divine Presence (who art in heaven), teaches us how to act morally towards each other (forgive us our trespasses as we forgive those who trespass against us) and invites us to live in the awareness of the present moment, (give us THIS DAY our daily bread), while also recognising the goal of all history in the revelation of the Kingdom (who IS in Heaven, thy Kingdom come, thy will be done on earth as it IS in heaven). The power of this prayer to deepen mindful awareness of Divine Presence and to initiate an ongoing relationship with Divine Love revealed as father is at the centre of the Christian prayer tradition.

In the sixth chapter of St Matthew we find the other passage of teaching on meditative prayer that Jesus give us. Here He speaks about the Pharisees when He tells his disciples that, when they pray, they should 'go into their inner room, close their door and pray to their Father in secret, and their Father, who sees what is done in secret, will reward them'.

We must remember that Jesus is speaking to first-century peasants, but He says to them to go to their 'inner room'. Most of them would have lived in one-room dwellings. So, was He telling them they needed to build an extension to pray? No, of course not.

He is using the language of the synagogue, of the time where the 'inner room' meant the 'heart' – to go to your inner room is to go to your heart.

'Close your door', means to close off all distractions so we can become attentive to the heart and presence of God within us.

So far, so good.

But it is at this point that the teaching becomes something new. Jesus tells them to 'pray to their Father in secret', to pray to God who is already there within their hearts. You are not calling God in from somewhere else. You are meeting God in God's house! The heart is God's dwelling place, His desired temple. He is already there and He sees you choosing to enter into prayer. He sees what is done in secret and will reward you with the life and grace of the Holy Spirit within.

What are we rewarded with?

We are rewarded with the grace of true awareness about the truth of who we are in God and before God.

That is Christian teaching in a nutshell. That is our contemplative tradition and the essence of the teaching of Jesus.

The Path of Meditative Prayer

The Hebrew word for prayer is *tefillah* and its core meaning is an existential connectedness to God that cannot be broken.

When I am meditating, I am tuning in to my fundamental connectedness to Divine Love. Another word also used to describe the action of praying is *lithphalel*, which means 'to become aware', to watch yourself in the mind-ful sense. It really means to see yourself in the light of Divine Presence, to come to see the truth of who you are.

So, praying becomes a fundamental, conscious connection to God that enables me to see who I am in His light. It enables my awareness of that fundamental connection to transform who I am – so I can grow into the person God would have me become.

That is the act of meditative prayer and its transforming power.

Transfiguration

In the gospels' account of the Transfiguration we get a glimpse of this transformation. The event of the transfiguration is the wonderful story about how, just before His passion, Jesus was accompanied to the mountaintop by the closest of His disciples. On the mountain, He is transfigured before them. They see the light of His divinity and they hear the Father's voice and perceive the presence of the Spirit. Moses and Elijah are also present, and poor old Peter is so overcome that he wants to stay there for ever – well, wouldn't you?

This piece of scripture and its traditional Byzantine icon were often given to beginners in meditative prayer in the eastern orthodox monasteries and they were asked a question to sit with during their meditation: 'On the mountain, who changed?'

The good novice, knowing their scripture well, would say, 'Jesus changed.'

The good abbot would smile and say, 'Go back and read it again.'

Of course, the answer that makes itself known after some reflection is that it is the disciples who are changed because they saw reality as it actually is. They were with Jesus in the Divine Present and saw His glory and His union with the Father and the Holy Spirit, and the fullness of the revelation that proceeds from God through the prophets Moses and Elijah.

But that's who Jesus is always, so when we walk up the mountain of meditation, we're called to change not who God is but who *we* are before God. We begin to have an awareness of reality and, in that awareness, we are transformed.

The Monastic Art of Mindful Attention

A couple of centuries after Christ, as we move towards a more Greek-speaking Church, there is the beginning of the monastic tradition in the deserts of Egypt.

Those first Desert Fathers and Mothers, as we call them, spoke of this quality of living with constant mindful attention towards God as *proseuchai* (turning attention towards praying with awareness) and later *nepsis* (interior watchfulness). They believed these were the essential qualities of all meditative prayer – namely the ability to be mindful and aware of God on a moment-by-moment basis, so that your whole life becomes a prayer and the command to 'pray always' (Thess 5:16-18) is at last fulfilled.

If you were a novice monk out there in the desert, you would have spent the first years of your training arriving to a state of mindful awareness of the presence of God, by practising the art of attention to God both within and without, while attempting to bring your soul to a place of restful awareness in the present moment.

These same practices deepen our own prayer and enable it to become both truly relational and an ongoing encounter with God. Once more, we find that the fruit of such living is not just awareness itself, but compassion that then reaches out to our brothers and sisters in their need and comes to see in every person – indeed in every being – the presence of God.

In Buddhism, the Buddha taught mindfulness as *sati*, a word derived from the Pali language meaning 'recollection of mind' or 'awareness'. He taught that this was an essential prerequisite for all other meditation and prayer practices.

This quality of being present would then invite the monk or the nun or the practitioner into the quality of attending, of being present to the self in its essential truth, as being an invitation to deeper and deeper levels of awareness.

This, in the Buddhist tradition, was to produce what they call 'single-pointed consciousness', the ability to focus completely on the present moment. It was this quality that developed compassion and awareness that would eventually bear fruit in the experience of enlightenment.

In this regard, all the great religious traditions are similar because they all start by teaching that to enter into reality fully, we must start with mindful attention. They all begin with the idea that the present moment has something revelatory about it.

There is the idea that the transcendent – what as

Christians we call the Divine – is both accessed and met moment by moment through this awareness. This is what, today, we would call mindfulness.

Religious traditions go off in different ways and they teach many different things and their goals can be different, but the important thing for us to become aware of is that they all begin in the same place as far as meditative practice is concerned.

Parallel though separate traditions coming from different and distant places with differing ideas and very often essentially different goals, yet they all exhibit the same idea: that if you want to be a human being fully alive and awake, then you must go deeper. You begin by attending to the present; you begin by finding a way to awareness that can calm the storms of distraction and stop you being concerned by anxiety about the future or the past.

Poetry Pause

Transfiguration

Transfiguration
happens
in each moment.
When a sunbeam cuts
through the forest canopy
and illumines a glade with

sudden glory,
transfiguration
happens.
When a flower unfurls
and startles
with stunning
colour,
transfiguration
happens.
When stillness settles
in the soul,
long enough for us
to notice light leaking
lovingly
into the world through
leaves, and
life quietly working
miracles of
resurrection from
the mulch
of seeming
death,
transfiguration
happens.
And even
when we,
worried,
busied
and bothered,

do not
notice our daily
divine draw
up the
mountain,
from glory
to
glory,
transfiguration
happens
still.

Christian Mindfulness: A Journey into Divine Presence

The great and essential difference in the Christian tradition when compared with many other religions and philosophies is the belief that we are not alone in this search for meaning, for a deeper and more fully awake human life. We believe that the love of God reveals itself to us constantly in creation, in history, in our hearts and, in the most definitive, final and universal sense, in the person of Jesus.

But how can we live in this mindful awareness of God in each moment? How can we meditate in such a way that we access this presence of love that exists in the calm centre of our being far beyond the touch of the storms of life?

Fortunately, the Christian tradition proposes very

simple and practical ways to come into contact with God. However, before we look at those ways, let's make sure we understand what we mean, in a Christian sense, when we speak of things like 'prayer', 'meditation' and even 'mindfulness'.

The Language of the Christian Prayer Tradition

When it comes to talking about prayer, meditation, contemplation, etc., there is often a confusion about what each word means. Often, this confusion is born out of the fact that people can become very confused when one teacher speaks of 'contemplation' and another speaks of 'meditation' to describe a similar thing.

For example, I remember meeting someone who, on learning that I taught meditation, said to me, 'Oh that meditation stuff is great. I've never felt better since I started meditating.'

'Great,' I said. 'So what are you doing in the meditation classes?'

'Well', they said, 'we lie on the ground and we relax and we relax and we relax, and, suddenly, you just kind of float away and then, after about twenty minutes, they ring a bell, and you're back and it feels great!'

'Of course, it does,' I said. 'That's called sleep.'

Now, while it is, of course, very important to have a relaxation element within our meditation – and we will be stressing the importance of deep relaxation as part of our meditation later – in the Christian understanding, meditation is not just about relaxation, as nice as it is to relax!

In fact, there are many other constitutive elements to our practice that should be understood and that's why clarity of language is so important.

Fortunately, over the course of the 2,000 years of Christianity (building, of course, on the 4,000-year foundation of Judaism), our tradition has been very clear about the different aspects and states of prayer, and the ways in which they are related.

However, today, it can get very confusing. You'll see people offering courses in contemplation, relaxation, stress release, mindfulness and even in focusing or simply attention – and it's easy to become confused.

So let us begin by clearing all this up. The first thing to say is that, in Christianity, mindfulness isn't the goal: it's simply a methodology to bring us closer to God. It uses a quality of human awareness of the present moment to enable a deepening of our attentiveness to God.

Mindfulness, then, is simply a human quality of awareness of the present moment. It is not in or of itself Christian, Buddhist, Hindu or anything else. It is simply a human quality of awareness and any human being of any faith – or none – can practise it to deepen their awareness of their own life.

However, many of the great prayer teachers of the

Christian tradition – people like the Desert Fathers, St Francis of Assisi, St Teresa of Ávila and St Francis de Sales to name but a few – have especially taught that this awareness, to help us encounter Christ in the present moment, was necessary and even sacramental. It needed to be established as part of our prayer discipline to prepare us for deep, meditative prayer and contemplation.

Mindfulness in our tradition is a human quality of awareness that we sanctify by making it a defining quality of our meditative practice.

So, when you see an athlete out on the field and they are totally in the zone, they are being mindful. When you see a poet or an artist standing in front of their canvas or with their blank piece of paper and they are completely focused on their inspiration, they are being mindful. When you see a mother or a father giving their complete attention to their child, they are being mindful. They are all human beings and they are being mindful.

In Christianity, however, we know we can go deeper again. In those mindful moments, we can discover an invitation to prayer, to a dialogue that slowly raises us to a place of rest and healing, a place of encountering the transcendent presence of God, so that God can begin to act in us. That is when the power of contemplation begins to happen.

Practice: Practising Mindfulness

To really see what this is like let's just practice a little moment of mindful meditation, shall we?

Find a comfortable seat in a quiet space, place your feet flat on the floor and your back comfortably straight, take a moment to settle yourself and simply pause.

A moment of awareness.

You don't need to move your posture.

You don't need to change anything.

You just need to be as you are but to be aware of yourself as you are.

So just check in with yourself.

How is your body at the moment?

Your body might have information for you right in this moment that you're not picking up as you read.

How is your body?

How are your emotions at the moment?

What is happening with your feelings at the moment?

How are your thoughts?

Where is your attention being pulled to at the moment?

Just notice any of the stimuli that cross the field of your attention.

Take a few moments to watch them go by.

And then, to draw yourself into this present moment, just be aware of your body as it connects to the chair you are sitting in as you read.

The feeling of the chair beneath you.

Become aware of the movement of the air in the room.

The movement of the air over your face or hands.

Finally, be just aware of your own breath.

Not changing the rhythm of the breath in any way.

Just notice your breath.

The first thing you did when you came into this world was to breathe in.

The very last thing you do before you leave this world will be to breathe out.

Rest in the awareness that we exist between the in-breath and the out-breath.

Just be aware of the breath, of this breath, of this moment as divine gift.

Each moment, each breath a gift from God.

And, just for a moment, rest in gratitude for your breath, for your life, in this present moment.

And then return to looking around you, to your feet on the floor.

Feel your back in the chair.

Well done. It can be as simple as that – just checking in. We make contact with the present moment and, through it, we can also connect to the fullness of our reality and then to God that holds reality in being.

From Mindfulness to Prayer

Prayer is the raising of the mind and the heart to God. So, it is focusing and attending, but it is also dialogic. It has two sides and is a relational experience. There is God and us. Prayer is a dialogue with God – it is part of our conversation, our relationality, with God and it transforms us.

It's also meant to be a transformative experience, during which the Holy Spirit present in our souls slowly changes us more and more into the likeness of Christ. So we are more and more incorporated (literally become one flesh) within the body of Christ (Rom 8:26). We become more and more a person in whom others will encounter Divine Love.

Traditionally, beginning in the desert theology of the third and fourth centuries CE, this was known as the 'Process of Theosis'. Through prayer and grace, we become as alike to God as it is possible for us to become, while still remaining perfectly human.

Of course, a real dialogue requires input from both parties. It also needs, among other things, a concerned openness, honesty, awareness of the other and, above all else, the ability to listen.

But what's our prayer very often like?

A storm of worries, words and wants! We talk, talk, talk, talk, talk, talk, talk, talk, talk and then we go away! Afterwards we say, 'I don't know what it is about prayer, it's doing nothing for me. I can never hear the voice of God or receive guidance.'

Of course you can't. You wouldn't expect a friend to be your friend without mutual listening, would you?

Listening, stillness, silence – these have to be part of our dialogue. Silence and stillness are at the heart of our prayer practice. If we are not still, we will never know (cf. Ps 96).

Poetry Pause

Silence, Stillness, Peace

Silence
is not
the
mere absence
of noise
but the
awareness
of the
Word
that thunders
in
the void.
Stillness
is not
the

mere absence
of movement
but the
awareness
of the
Fire
from which
all that is
arises.
Peace
is not
the mere absence
of conflict
but the
awareness
of the
One
who is.
Be Silent.
Be Still.
Be Peace.
Be
and
you will
know.

Chapter 4

Meditation in the Christian Tradition

In the Christian tradition, meditation is understood as a form of prayer that may be either discursive (sometimes called active) or passive (sometimes called quiet). In discursive meditation, our imagination and our intellect are active and help us to understand elements of faith, such as when we meditate on the mysteries of the Rosary or on a passage of scripture or on a teaching of a saint.

Lectio Divina – the ancient art of considering a passage of scripture in a quiet and meditative way, which we'll come to later in this chapter – is a good example of this, as this particular form of scriptural meditation, in its first steps at least, is discursive meditation.

Your mind is working with the message of the scripture, your intellect is working to understand and relate the passage to your life, and your imagination is working in both picturing the scene being read and in looking forward to applying the lessons you have learned in your future life.

Passive meditation on the other hand, means simply resting in deep awareness of the presence of God. St Teresa of Ávila, that great master of prayer, referred to this in *The Way of Perfection* as the 'prayer of quiet' or 'the prayer of calm abiding'.

It should be noted that our tradition teaches us that both forms of meditative prayer are necessary.

Discursive meditation is supposed to lead us into passive meditation – into stillness, into quiet being with God.

As the great St John Vianney quoted in *The Little Catechism of the Cure of Ars* when he was asked what this form of prayer was like: 'I look at Him and He looks at me.' This meditative gazing is the mutual regard of love, a resting in peace together that may have no overt emotional content or may even be simply spent returning over and over again to the presence of God from distractions (as we will see later, the distractions may even be said to be part of the prayer practice). We are gazing upon God with mindful awareness or returning our attention after we became distracted. We are gazing on the One who is always gazing upon us as His beloved.

Contemplation

Discursive and passive meditation, in turn, lead us to contemplation. Contemplation is the goal of all meditation and prayer. When we are in this state, we enter into an even deeper stillness and silence of body, mind and soul than simple meditation may ever produce. In contemplation, the Divine is acting in us in a transformative way and we are passive.

This is an unmerited grace – a free gift of Divine Love – and while we can work at being contemplative, in creating the conditions in our lives that makes contemplation more readily possible, we cannot induce this state.

In meditation, we know that we are active even in the passive forms.

In contemplation, God is active and we are stilled.

In all of our practice of mindfulness and meditation, in all of our prayer practices, we strive to become contemplative – in other words to create the best conditions to facilitate the experience of contemplation.

We have many contemplative practices, of which mindfulness is a fundamental one, to create the space in which contemplation may happen. But we must always remember that contemplation is God's work in us.

There's a lovely story from the monastic tradition that illustrates this beautifully.

A young novice, who was in the midst of training in all of his meditative and mindful prayer, went to his Abba, his elder, and he said, 'Abba, look I am doing everything that you told me. I'm doing all the prayer and all the prostrations, and I'm praying and meditating on the Psalms, and I'm reflecting on the scriptures and attending the Holy Eucharist and I'm doing my manual work and I'm trying to be kind to the brothers. I'm doing all of the practices but nothing is really happening yet.'

The Abba looked at him with great love and understanding and said, 'Come with me.'

They walked in silence up a mountain and watched the sun slowly setting in the west. Then the Abba turned to the novice and said, 'Brother, if you tried really hard, could you prevent the sun from rising in the morning?'

The novice looked surprised and said, 'No, of course I couldn't. No matter how much I try, I couldn't prevent the sun from rising.'

'Exactly,' said the Abba. 'And no matter how hard you try or don't try, God's grace will eventually rise in your soul.'

So, the novice asked the question that you're all asking in your head right now: 'But, Abba, if this is so, then why am I doing all the prayer and meditation stuff? If it's going to happen anyway, why do all the work?'

The old Abba looked at him with love and said, 'So that you may be awake to see the sun rise.'

All roads lead back to the cultivation of awareness.

So, we pray and we meditate. We begin to drop our distractions so that we arrive at the point where we will notice, in the moment it happens, the movement of the inspiration of unmerited grace and surrender to it.

All our meditative practices are done to create this atmosphere, stability and discipline, so that we can attend to the movement of God's presence and spirit when it happens.

Otherwise, like the gentle breeze of God's presence that Elijah could only discern when the storms and earthquakes and howling winds had abated (1 Kings), we could miss the moment of Divine Encounter.

After all, how often have we looked back and realised we missed the moment?

I missed the inspiration.

I lost the opportunity.

I should have been more aware.

I should have been more present.

This is the storm of self-recrimination that we are all so often consumed by. In these moments, we must remember that all of our meditative practices are to stabilise us in an encounter with the present moment, to enable us to catch the inspiration of Divine Love when it comes to us and to surrender to it, to be transformed by it, to become more Christ-like so that, eventually, it is not us who lives, but Christ who lives in us (Gal 2:20).

There are very rich concepts within this understanding, far more than we can go into here. Our Desert Fathers and Mothers taught that the essence of the practice is to become aware of the connection with God and to dwell in that connection every day.

There is a lovely story that illustrates this.

One of the novices of the desert was feeling in need of a recalibration in his prayer life. He went to see the Abba and said, 'Abba, I've come for a word.'

The Abba smiled and said, 'Awareness!'

The novice said, 'I've come a long way, is there anything more than that?'

'Yes', said the Abba. 'Awareness. Awareness. Awareness!' And he closed the door on the novice.

This may seem a severe response at first, but it's a direct way of teaching that, without building awareness of fundamental truth, there is no entering into contemplative transformation.

St Francis speaks of this as well in his admonitions in that lovely statement, 'For what a person is before God, that he is and no more.'

In other words, when we stand before God in meditation, we see the truth of ourselves, but we are not lost in that moment – we are lifted up by love and say, 'Here I am. Here is my truth, Lord. Transform me, change me, let me grow.'

As St Teresa of Ávila says, 'Prayer is simply this, a conversation with someone whom I already know loves me. I have nothing to prove.'

It is not: 'Dear Lord, did you see me yesterday? Wasn't it wonderful when I looked after so-and-so?'

And it's certainly not the other extreme of: 'Dear Lord, I'm a terrible, horrible person, how could you possibly forgive me?'

Instead, it is simply: 'Dear Lord, here I am.'

That's it. 'Here I am.' But within that 'Here I am' there is gaze upon gaze, light upon light, and we are invited ever more deeply into communion with the Divine and, in that communion, we are changed.

From Simple Mindfulness to Spiritual Attention

So how do we move into this mindful attention of Divine Presence that changes us and enables us to grow more deeply into the image of God?

Let's go to St Simeon, one of the great fathers of Christian contemplative practice. Known as the 'new theologian', he wrote about attention as being as necessary in your spiritual life as breath in your physical life. This is mindful attention (to the self in God in the moment).

Simeon saw that when Jesus gave us the Beatitudes, He said, 'Blessed are the pure in heart for they shall see God.' Jesus was not just talking about a moral purity; it was very clear to His disciples that He was speaking about the purity of hearts, the purity of our awareness of the mind and heart on God.

St Simeon went on to teach that if you do not have attention in yourself, you cannot be pure in heart and cannot become pure in spirit. You cannot weep and be contrite, nor be gentle and meek, nor hunger and thirst after righteousness, nor be merciful nor a peacemaker, nor suffer persecution for righteousness sake. For St Simeon, the life of the Beatitudes is the life of meditative awareness – and it all begins with attending to the presence of God in the present moment.

A friend of mine is a wonderful teacher and a great Christian. On one occasion when I was visiting her school, I met her in the staff room and she told me she had decided to take a career break. I was sorry to see her go and said so.

She told me she had realised that very day that she definitely needed to take a break, so naturally I asked what had happened. Her response makes me smile to this day. She said she had been teaching the students the Beatitudes and had asked each of them to memorise a Beatitude. They were to go around the classroom and each student said their Beatitude out loud, like a chorus of Beatitudes!

Unfortunately, one child just didn't take it seriously and was making up Beatitudes, changing them for comic effect and disrupting the class.

Then, she said, 'Suddenly, I found myself on the

corridor with this student and I was repeating into their face, "Blessed are the merciful!" The student just raised one eyebrow at me, and I realised right then that I needed to take a career break.'

A beautiful example of coming to mindful awareness in the moment!

The Beatitudes from the Gospel of Matthew (Mt 5:1-12) then are our code to our way of being with others, but they are born from that purity of heart that enables us to see God in, with and through others. So often we put it the other way around, we try and live the Beatitudes, we try and 'do' the Beatitudes, and then we become frustrated when other people don't do the Beatitudes the way we do the Beatitudes – and we fall into egoic judgement. Let's pause with them for a moment.

Practice: The Beatitudes

Traditionally, meditating on the Beatitudes may be seen as a wonderful way of examining our lives for the fruits of mindful living. So, for a few moments I invite you to make yourself comfortable. Find a comfortable seat in a quiet space, place your feet flat on the floor and your back comfortably straight, take a moment to settle yourself and simply pause. Try to sit alert and aware, while allowing the breath to anchor you in the present moment. Gently watching the breath and the ebb and flow of its inward and outward path. When you feel you have entered into stillness, then gently read the Beatitudes as given below. You may want to read them more than once.

Now when He saw the crowds, he went up on a mountainside and sat down. His disciples came to Him, and He began to teach them, saying:

Blessed are the poor in spirit, for theirs is the kingdom of heaven.

Blessed are those who mourn, for they will be comforted.

Blessed are the meek, for they will inherit the earth.

Blessed are those who hunger and thirst after righteousness, for they will be filled.

Blessed are the merciful, for they shall be shown mercy.

Blessed are the pure in heart, for they will see God.

Blessed are the peacemakers, for they will be called the children of God.

Blessed are those who are persecuted because of righteousness, for theirs is the kingdom of heaven.

Blessed are you when people insult you, persecute you and falsely say all kinds of evil against you because of me. Rejoice and be glad, because great is your reward in heaven, for in the same way they persecuted the prophets who were before you.

If you are alone, it can be a help to read them aloud. However you read them, read them slowly. Allow each word to sound deeply in your heart. When you have read them slowly and gently you may begin to ask yourself which Beatitude is calling for my attention? Which is challenging me or inviting me to look a little deeper at my own life? Feel free to spend time with the one or the few that called for your attention. Are there any situations in your life where living the Beatitudes would invite change?

Receive the blessing of their words of guidance. And then when you are ready, read them once more before returning to the awareness of the breath for three cycles of in-breath and out-breath and then finish with an act of gratitude.

Into the Desert

To understand the deepening of our mindfulness into full spiritual attention, we must move to the desert for while, specifically the deserts of Egypt and Libya. It was here around the year 300 CE that there was an extraordinary movement within Christianity where meditative practice began to move out to the edges, to the periphery.

A group of men and women formed who felt a call to the desert, to a place of solitude so they could dwell completely with God in prayer. They became known as the Desert Fathers and Mothers.

Perhaps the most famous of these early monastic souls, and the one who, to this day, is considered the archetype of the monastic search, is St Antony of Egypt, also known as Abba Antony the Great, or simply as the Father of Monks. He went into the desert having heard the call to give everything to God.

His story becomes the archetypal journey into attentive stillness. Recorded by St Athanasius, it became a spiritual classic, and I would urge anyone wishing to understand meditative awareness to read it.

When we first meet him, St Antony is a Christian, a member of a wealthy family and about eighteen. Sadly, both his parents were killed in an accident. We don't know what the accident was, we are just told they died, and Antony and his sister were orphaned, though at least they were somewhat comfortably off. Normally, this would be something to give thanks for, a small mercy after a great tragedy, but, for Antony, this sudden shock sent him into a kind of a worrying spin around the great question we must all ask at some point in our lives: What is life really about when it can be taken away so quickly?

We find this often in our own spiritual lives. It's often in a crisis that we hear the Spirit of God for the first time.

It's very true: when we are in pain, we very often feel His presence or hear His word for the first time in a clear way.

That is what happened to Antony. The finery of his life no longer had any lustre, and he began to pray. While walking through the streets of Egypt, he went into a little church and heard the priest proclaim the gospel of the rich, young man – in which Christ tells the young man that if you would be perfect, you must go sell all that you own and then come follow me (Mt 19:21).

Antony was electrified! He sold most of his things, though he left a little bit of money for his sister, and went into the desert. However, he was troubled that he hadn't given everything away, so he went back to Egypt, took the money from his sister, put her into a community of Christian women and then went back into the desert, once and for all. History remains silent about what the sister thought of this, but I imagine not very much.

In his later years, Antony talked about the extremes of youth, and that he needed to balance out his action later in his life.

However, when he was in the desert – and having received instruction from St Paul of Egypt, one of the early hermits he met there – he created a pattern of life that is the essence of all religious life. All monastic communities trace their family tree back to Antony and to those first Desert Fathers and Mothers of the third to fifth centuries.

So, what was their practice? How do they live this life of mindful attentiveness to Divine Love, this work to live in the awareness of Divine Presence as taught by St Antony?

St Augustine tells us one of their core practices was

'arrow prayers'. These were short simple prayers, often only a line or two, sometimes even spoken aloud, that were 'fired like arrows to heaven' to keep them consciously connected with the presence of God.

They would use these short prayers so that they could pray as they worked at their chores in order to keep their awareness and equanimity of soul between the periods of deeper prayer and meditation. They were often just the repetition of the name of Jesus or a line from scripture, and they would keep this going almost like chewing gum of the mind. It was a way of being aware of God in the midst of their work.

This is something we can do too – it's one of the easiest of spiritual practices! In fact, many of us did this in the past without even knowing.

When people ask me who my first meditation teacher was, they expect me to name a monk or nun or one of the friars of the order. They are surprised to hear that my first teacher of the practices of meditation, even though I didn't know it at the time, was my gran, my mother's mother.

Because my grandmother lived her prayers constantly. Whenever I went to visit her, she'd be busy cleaning or cooking or whatever was the duty of the moment, but, if you listened very closely, you would hear her say over and over: 'Sacred Heart of Jesus, I place all my trust in Thee', 'Jesus may your kingdom come', 'Jesus mercy, Mary help'. That was the music of her life. (She was half-deaf, so she didn't know she was saying this prayer out loud.)

Of course, if I had mentioned 'meditation' or the 'prayer of calm abiding' to her, she wouldn't have known what I was talking about. But she was in the practice fully. This is a reminder that the deepest contemplatives and meditators we will meet are often those who invite us into an awareness of the presence of God in the present moment.

A friar who lives in Galway and who is now a hermit told me that on one occasion, when he was a schoolboy, he came home to find his mother spring cleaning. All the windows were open, all the doors were open, and he thought, *Oh no, I'm going to be helping here now for the day*. But as he arrived in, he could hear his mother chatting to somebody in the kitchen so he thought she must have a visitor. However, when he walked in, he found his mother was all by herself. So, he asked her, 'Who are you talking to?'

'Mary,' she replied.

'Mary from down the road?' he asked.

'No!' she laughed. 'Mary from heaven!'

This is the habitual awareness of the Divine Presence that we aspire to, and this is how those early brothers and sisters lived. They repeated their arrow prayers – those short little prayers or one-liners that connected them to the presence of God – which are so important as touchstones of spiritual connection with God.

From Arrows to Mantras

The second form of prayer that those early monks and nuns worked with was what became known as the *versiculum* (little word). Today, in the Christian tradtition we call this the 'prayer word' or 'mantra', made popular by the methods taught by the World Community of Christian Meditation, an organisation founded by the Benedictine John Main, and then further deepened within the broader Centering Prayer movement founded by two Cistercian monks, Fr Thomas Keating and Fr Basil Pennington.

However, going back to the early desert tradition, as exemplified in the works of those desert monks, those who succeeded St Antony, people like St John Climacus and Evagrius Ponticus and others, the practice is simple – it's the idea of sitting in deep stillness but allowing a short phrase of scripture, or a holy word or one of the divine titles, to be the focus that holds your mind anchored in the Divine Presence, while you wait on the movement towards contemplative experience.

This practice is often used for stable sitting meditation. But, of course, the problem is that when we sit, even with the help of the word, we often find that our minds are scattered and distracted.

Evagrius Ponticus was one of the early Desert Fathers who created a wonderful little book – *The Praktike* – that is still studied today. It was written as a guide for monks and nuns about how to deal with their thoughts in meditation. It is still as relevant as it was when he wrote it because he realised that when somebody tells you to sit still, be quiet and think of nothing – what happens is absolute chaos.

I've met people who have been turned off meditation because they have been introduced to it incorrectly. They are told to just sit and be, and then the horrors arise within! We scoot off into the past, we run away forwards into the future, we fantasise, we think about things, crazy things that seem to arrive from nowhere. The Desert Fathers and Mothers described these thoughts as mosquitoes. It's a wonderful image, isn't it?

We all know what it's like. You are sitting looking at a beautiful view and you're restful and at ease, considering just the view in front of you. You are totally in the moment and then, suddenly, your mind flits back to something that happened earlier in the day. You are not focused on the view anymore, and so the little thoughts arrive and disturb you as you follow them off along the path, forgetting where you are meant to be.

Evagrius spoke to a lot of the early Desert Fathers and Mothers and asked them how they dealt with these thoughts. The answer was the *versiculum*. You give your mind something to focus on and, eventually, all images and thoughts fall away, and you are left in stillness and silence – but you need to be able to return to the word as an anchor in meditation.

In the Buddhist tradition, they speak of this experience of the chaos of thought as the 'monkey mind'. The mind that is always looking at something else and is always distracted – whatever you call the experience, it exists. It is simply part of our inability to be ourselves or be in the present moment, and to be with God in the present moment as fully as possible.

The Posture of Meditation

This leads us neatly along to our bodily postures when we meditate. These, too, were considered to be extremely important in the meditative prayer of the desert. The Desert Fathers and Mothers used various forms of bowing, prostrations and genuflections to keep themselves alert and aware in the Divine Presence.

One form of this that spread right the way across the world and down through time into the Franciscan tradition as well is praying with your hands extended. In the Celtic countries, we called this the 'cross prayers' or the 'cross vigil'.

In the Irish tradition, there is a wonderful story illustrating the power of this form of meditative posture from the life of St Kevin of Glendalough.

The story goes that as Kevin prayed in his stone cell in the woods above Glendalough, he would stretch his hands out of the windows of the cell because it was so small. During one session of deep prayer, he was so absorbed in his meditation that a blackbird built its nest in one of his upwards-cupped hands and there laid her eggs. When he came back to himself and saw what had happened, Kevin prayed that he would be absorbed in contemplation again until the eggs were hatched.

The simple reason for these postures is to keep your mind awake and focused. For example, when you meditate with your arms extended and become tired, your arms begin to drop and ache, and you realise your focus has been broken.

I knew of one lady who was beginning meditative practice but would often find herself sleeping. As a remedy, she would sit on her chair to meditate but she would hold her keys in her hand and so, if she began to nod off, she would drop the keys and hear the bang on the floor.

People often begin by asking me if there is a particular posture that they should adopt for meditation, and the answer is simply to allow yourself to be in an alert, relaxed position.

There are a few traditional postures that were used within the desert and, later within the monasteries, that are still used to this day. But, as different as they are, they all aim at a relaxed awareness of your body to assist in focusing your attention on God.

The Christian tradition has always recognised that we are psycho-biological wholes and so what is happening in your body has an effect on your mind and soul, and vice versa. We are illumined in prayer in both body and soul.

The first type of posture we will look at is kneeling, either simply on the knees with the upper legs and back straight. (This looks like what you would think of as traditional Christian prayer posture.) The problem with this, however, is that, without support, and definitely without much repetition, this posture can become painful and tiring quite quickly.

A variation of it that works very well is the second posture for meditation. This time, we kneel but with the sitting back, leaning on the calves. Again, without a lot of work this can become painful, but it is much easier to maintain alert aware focus in this position. The distracting elements of this posture may be alleviated by placing what is known as a prayer stool, a small flat wooden support over your calves that raises your thighs from the calves, supports your backside and tilts your pelvis slightly forwards to keep your back straight. This is a posture I would recommend to the beginner. Should your legs or shins and knees be especially sensitive, then a rubber exercise mat or folded blanket may also be put on the ground to support you further.

The third posture that is often referred to in the monastic literature is simply to sit on a small stool or chair, near the ground, with your back straight and your hands resting on your lap.

Finally, the fourth, is the simple cross-legged position that, today, is often associated with things like yoga or Eastern forms of meditation. This form has always been used in the Christian tradition, and if you are used to it, then it can enable you to sustain long periods of deep practice. However, if you are not used to this form of posture, my advice would be to leave it aside because, without practice, it is the one that can cause pain and discomfort that is really difficult to focus past.

In the end, you should simply choose a position that is comfortable, where you are relaxed, awake and aware. A posture that enables your breath to move in an unrestrained way is needed. In order to enable this more easily, the posture that is adopted should be one in which your knees are slightly lower than your pelvis, if possible. This is why the prayer-stool posture is one that is very helpful to the beginner.

So, when people say to me, 'I'm beginning meditation, should I start by discovering if I can fold myself up into a place on the floor?' I always say absolutely not because, within five minutes, your legs will start burning and then your back will start burning, and your meditation will be taken up with the burning!

A comfortable, relaxed chair with a straight back is fine, as long as you are able to place your feet firmly on the floor, with your hands relaxed and open, which, in our tradition of meditation, is simply a nice image of being open to the presence of the Holy Spirit.

If you have a bad back or are sick or in pain, and you need to lie down to meditate, that is fine – however, if you are able, you should draw your feet towards your chest; then, if you begin to fall asleep, your knees will fall to the side, which will bring you back to awareness and you will have a way to teach yourself a slightly different way of meditating.

What should be understood clearly, though, is that these postures are not magical. They facilitate our practice, but they do not cause anything in us or around us. They are merely practical techniques learned over centuries of trial and error by our monastic forefathers and foremothers who taught us what helps them attain relaxed aware focus on the presence of the Divine, so that we may do the same. In other words, how to arrive at a state of being that fulfilled the command to pray always.

Leading to Lectio

There are many different ways of being present. All of the practices of the Desert Fathers and Mothers show that their understanding of the spiritual life was a holistic one – involving the mind, heart and soul.

The heart, the emotions, the thoughts were dealt

with through spiritual direction and, from there, their Abba or their Amma – the father or the mother of their thoughts – would offer ways to deal with whatever distractions or temptations were disturbing their life of unity with God.

The other great practice that they handed down to us is Lectio Divina – the 'Divine' or meditative reading of scripture. Lectio Divina is encountering scripture as a prayerful meditation with God. It is not scripture study per se: this is actually sitting with the word as an encounter with Divine Love.

The scriptures are seen as a conduit of Divine Love and this became the quintessential practice of the monastic life as a way of encountering the presence of God. Later, it would be formalised into various stages, the first of which was relaxation – you don't go straight to the scripture.

You need to come back to yourself; you need to let go of the day and be present. They would use the tools of mindful awareness and the prayer word as a way of coming into a stable awareness of the presence of God.

Secondly you hear the word. You don't just read it – you hear it. If possible, you read it aloud (if you are in the presence of others, then maybe you need to read it quietly), but if at all possible, you speak the passage aloud.

The word needs to be spoken. It was meant to be spoken and heard – and, sometimes, you hear in the speaking what you haven't heard in the reading. This is especially true today when, because of social media, we all tend to scan things quickly.

The next stage of the practice is the repetition of the word. Having read the passage of scripture a few times, both aloud and in silence, and having sat with it for a while, you wait and see what part of the scripture passage – what line or even single word – particularly catches your attention and resonates with your life in that present moment. Arriving at this point is to arrive at an inner doorway of the heart, opening into the presence of God. You begin to repeat the line or word either aloud or in your mind.

At first, there is the search for the meaning of the phrase and the seeking of resonance but, as the repetition continues, there is a sinking into silence where conceptual thought ceases and there is just the word and the breath in action.

The Celtic monks called this 'chewing the cud' of scripture, seeing in it a parallel to the cattle in the field. You have eaten the grass (read the word), but you chew and chew in repetition before you swallow it, until your mind moves and the silence is lost and so you bring the phrase or word of scripture back up into your mind and, in returning to repetition, you chew it some more.

In this way, like the cow chewing the cud, we get all of the goodness from the scripture and then, finally, a deep silence falls. In that moment, we wait for what the ancients called the 'harp of the heart' to be plucked, for a very small moment of profound awareness to dawn.

Yes, the harp of the heart is plucked, and we become aware of the word as a living reality within us, a conduit of God and a place of encounter with the transcendent meaning of reality. Then, we can make the phrase or word of scripture our *versiculum*, the repetition of the word internally, as our mantra for the day, and we can take that word with us out into our offices or into our families and, in the midst of our day, we can return to it as a way of being present to the word.

Practice: Practising Lectio Divina

In the following pages are a few short passages from the New Testament that we can use to begin the practice of Lectio.

Begin in each case by settling with the scriptures in a quiet space where you won't be disturbed for twenty minutes.

Find a comfortable seat in a quiet space, place your feet flat on the floor and your back comfortably straight, take a moment to settle yourself and simply pause.

Take a moment to prepare to truly enter into the present moment as a place of sacred encounter with the Divine. You might like to light a candle or make a bow or the sign of the cross as a formal gesture to begin.

Inwardly invoke the Holy Spirit to help you discern Divine Presence in and through the passage of scripture.

Take a few moments to become still.

Come to the awareness of your breath and for a few moments rest in the rhythm of the in-breath and out-breath.

If possible then read the passage you choose aloud and slowly, twice.

Try and picture the scene described in the passage as clearly as possible.

Read the passage again and notice any word or phrase that seems to speak to your current reality, even if only by association.

Allow the phrase to sit with you, gently repeating it with the rhythm of your breath.

If distractions come, just notice them without becoming engaged and return to the phrase each time.

Allow the phrase to slowly sink into silence within.

If you wish you can return to another phrase or image and repeat the same steps again.

Finally, read the whole passage aloud again and end with a moment of thanksgiving.

The Healing of Blind Bartimaeus
(Mt 10:46–52)

They came to Jericho. As Jesus and His disciples and a large crowd were leaving Jericho, Bartimaeus son of Timaeus, a blind beggar, was sitting by the roadside. When he heard that it was Jesus of Nazareth, he began to shout out and say, 'Jesus, Son of David, have mercy on me!' Many sternly ordered him to be quiet, but he cried out even more loudly, 'Son of David, have mercy on me!' Jesus stood still and said, 'Call him here.' And they called the blind man, saying to him, 'Take heart; get up, He is calling you.' So throwing off his cloak, he sprang up and came to Jesus. Then Jesus said to him, 'What do you want me to do for you?' The blind man said to Him, 'My teacher, let me see again.' Jesus said to him, 'Go; your faith has made you well.' Immediately he regained his sight and followed him on the way.

Points to consider as a help to Lectio:

- See the scene as clearly as you can, the noise, the dust, the crowds, the presence of Jesus and the beggar on the road.

- Make the cry of the beggar your own, perhaps thinking about areas of blindness that may exist in your life.

- What would it be like to have clarity in these areas?

- Allow the cry of the beggar to become your mantra or *versiculum*.

- Trust in the desire of Jesus to heal your blindness.

The Wedding Feast of Cana (John 2:1–11)

On the third day there was a wedding in Cana of Galilee, and the mother of Jesus was there. Jesus and His disciples had also been invited to the wedding. When the wine ran out, the mother of Jesus said to Him, 'They have no wine.' And Jesus said to her, 'Woman, what concern is that to you and to me? My hour has not yet come.' His mother said to the servants, 'Do whatever He tells you.' Now standing there were six stone water jars for the Jewish rites of purification, each holding twenty or thirty gallons. Jesus said to them, 'Fill the jars with water.' And they filled them up to the brim. He said to them, 'Now draw some out, and take it to the chief steward.' So they took it. When the steward tasted the water that had become wine, and did not know where it came from (though the servants who had drawn the water knew), the steward called the bridegroom and said to him, 'Everyone serves the good wine first, and then the inferior wine after the guests have become drunk. But you have kept the good wine until now.' Jesus did this, the first of his signs, in Cana of Galilee, and revealed his glory; and his disciples believed in him.

Points to consider as a help to Lectio:

- See the scene as clearly as you can, the wedding, the embarrassment of the couple, the gentleness of Mary.

- Consider any area of your life in which you would like to see transformation.

- What water in your life needs to become wine?

- What would it be like if Mary spoke on your behalf to Jesus?

- Allow Mary's instruction 'Do whatever He tells you' to become your mantra, your *versiculum*.

- Ask yourself: 'What would my life be like if I did what He told me?'

The Parable of the Lost Sheep (Luke 15:1–7)

Now all the tax-collectors and sinners were coming near to listen to Him. And the Pharisees and the scribes were grumbling and saying, 'This fellow welcomes sinners and eats with them.' So He told them this parable: 'Which one of you, having a hundred sheep and losing one of them, does not leave the ninety-nine in the wilderness and go after the one that is lost until he finds it? When he has found it, he lays it on his shoulders and rejoices. And when he comes home, he calls together his friends and neighbours, saying to them, 'Rejoice with me, for I have found my sheep that was lost.'

Just so, I tell you, there will be more joy in heaven over one sinner who repents than over ninety-nine righteous people who need no repentance.

Points to consider as a help to Lectio:

- See the scene as clearly as you can, the two different groups surrounding Jesus.

- Consider any area of your life in which you feel the need for repentance or rescue.

- See the image of the Good Shepherd.

- Hear the phrase 'I have found my sheep that was lost' and let that become your mantra or *versiculum*.

- Make an act of trust in the presence of Jesus in your life as the Good Shepherd.

Silence and Reflection in Lectio Divina

In all of these moments of Lectio, make sure that there is at least an equal amount of time spent in attentive silence as there is in discursive thought.

Unfortunately, the time of reflective silence can often be a stage that is forgotten or not given enough importance by those who practise Lectio Divina either alone or in a group. Often, we read our piece of scripture and we read it again, and then we say what we thought about it and then go straight to petitionary prayer or fellowship, with only a little bit of silence during which we were thinking about the word in an intellectual or discursive manner.

We must remember that, without the silence, it is very difficult to encounter the presence.

We are practising not to understand – and certainly not to 'get through' – the scriptures in a particular space of time. We are practising to encounter and draw near to God at our heart and to yield to His love. For each of us, this will be a unique journey with unique timing. We are loved individually by God and every encounter is totally personal and unique.

To illustrate this, there's a lovely story of a great Franciscan master of prayer that speaks to this need for a meditative pacing in our practice of Lectio. He was teaching Lectio Divina to his students and the novices. They were using the text of the 'Our Father', the prayer of Jesus that He taught the disciples when they asked Him how they should pray.

The master was using this text as a way of training the students to this core practice of meditative prayer. Each day, they would meet and, each day, they brought up all their ideas and all their thoughts and reflections on the text. As he was listening, he seemed delighted that they were getting so much out of it.

Then, one of the students said, 'Father, how long have you been working with the "Our Father" as a text for Lectio?'

'For fourteen years,' he answered with a gentle smile.

They looked at him in shock! Fourteen years just with the 'Our Father'? Fourteen years, considering it, praying with it every day?

Finally, one of the students got up the courage to ask the next question: 'But, Father, if you've been working with the text for fourteen years, how far have you got in it?'

And the master said, 'Just as far as "Our" . . . just as far as "Our".'

At this, they nearly collapsed! 'Our' is the first word of the prayer! How could he possibly have spent fourteen years on the first word?

The master saw what was in their hearts and began to teach. 'Sons, for a moment just think. The Son of God, the second person of the Trinity, the One who is when all else is not, when teaching us to pray did not say 'My Father', as the disciples would have expected. No. He said 'Our' . . . and that is mystery enough for a lifetime, let alone for fourteen years.'

Other Somatic Elements of the Desert Tradition

Combined with the practice of the arrow prayers, the *versiculum* and Lectio, meditative practice often had a somatic or bodily element as well. The practices mentioned in the previous pages were often combined with particular postures like standing with arms outspread, prostrating upon the ground and most importantly with fasting. Many of the fathers and mothers of the monastic tradition were very clear that diet had an awful lot to do with meditation, and that just as there were times to eat there were also times to fast, especially when they wanted to stabilise their meditative practice or strengthen their quality of awareness. The practice of the Desert Fathers and Mothers, and of many monastic orders to this day, is almost exclusively vegetarian, at least during important times of the year or deeper periods of retreat. It was believed by some monastic teachers that as well as the giving up of meat being an act of discipline, it was also an act of compassion towards the animals that brought a clarity to the meditator's mind.

Another practice that untied body and mind was what they called *agrypna* (watching): this was keeping vigil through the middle of the night. Why? Because it's the quietest time, when there are no distractions. One of the gifts of this practice for us today, when so many people have sleep issues, is to realise that if you have insomnia already, you can think of it as a problem or perhaps think of it as a call to meditation, an invitation to spend time with God in the quiet of the night.

The next time you wake up and it's the middle of the night and you're wide awake, don't despair or be irritated or hurt. Instead say, 'OK, Lord, we will be together for a little while.' When you eventually return to sleep, you will find it much easier to rest deeply.

Poetry Pause

Holy Insomnia

There are those who sleep;
and
there are those who are called
to dwell
in the
divine in-between;
they go by many names:
Monks
Poets
Artists
Writers

Singers
Nuns
Fathers
Mothers
Lovers
Elders;
the sacred company of
holy insomniacs;
Ghosts all.
Those who stand at the
threshold places
keeping watch,
and know the deep pain of choice;
and the deepest pain
of being chosen.
Stitching together the
day and the night
with gentle attention
they
dwell in twilight
dusks,
and moth light,
and moonsets,
and predawn glows,
and scent the breezes
that carry
the grey hint of tomorrow's
storm;
sensations

that stir the heart and
calm
the
ever chattering
mind.
Walking in silence and
stillness
they can barely tell
who they are
let alone
why they are.
Only knowing divine purpose
and meaning
flowing through every moment
as love,
as fire,
as now.
Having tasted the failure of
Words,
they choose instead the
pure voice
of breath,
of tears,
of laughter,
until all becomes prayer.
They are those who
keep the world
together
watching over it

through
hours of night,
being a spark of hope
to the despairing,
being a spark of light
to those lost in their own
inner darkness,
simply being,
for those who have
no one to be for them,
simply
holding the darkness of
night
close enough,
long enough,
lovingly enough,
that it births
the dawn's
daily Divine gift
of
beginning,
with a burst
of
birdsong.

Chapter 5

The Practice of Attending

As we go a little deeper into our understanding of contemplative awareness and mindfulness, we can look a little more deeply at this idea of *kavanah*, of bringing the heart into attending to the presence of God in the present moment.

We can begin by recognising that this deep awareness is to respond to God in every present moment by cultivating an attitude of heart and mind which is best summed up in three words: 'Here I am.'

This powerful response occurs seventeen times in four canonical books of Hebrew scripture (Genesis, Exodus, Samuel and Isaiah). It says that I am present, attending, listening to the One who has called me.

As such, it is the essential quality of the person who would do the will of God in the present moment. Even when that person falls away or runs away from their calling, eventually, if they are open to listening to the heart of their own being, they will discern God and respond once again, 'Here I am.'

This call and response continues into the New Testament and reaches its acme in the response of Our Lady, 'Behold the handmaid of the Lord' – another and even more perfect way of saying, 'Here I am.' (It was the handmaid's role to attend upon the king, literally to watch and wait for his call to a moment of service.)

This response, locating yourself as being in the presence of God, is also to participate in the healing brought by the incarnation that, once again, enables human nature and divine nature to return to an intimacy lost in the Garden of Eden when, in answer to the first question of God to humanity, 'Where are you?', Adam and Eve hid in shame rather than pronounce in truth, 'Here I am.'

This, then, is the call of the human soul when fully placed before God in the present moment. It implies an attitude of mindful awareness, and the removal of the navel-gazing egoic life that occupies us all so very much.

It becomes the cry of those who have their attention on God. Those who are not worried about whether God is there, because God is always there. Instead, it's about you tuning into the presence, 'Here I am . . . Behold the handmaid of the Lord . . . Here I am!'

As we move towards that awareness, we learn that it begins to sanctify, to make us aware of the inherent holiness of the moment. So, while mindfulness is often understood today mainly in a Buddhist context, we know that it has always been present in the Judeo-Christian tradition. As we have said, it's the essential quality of all prayer and meditation, and it shows us that there is no aspect of our lives that may not be a sacramental moment, a place of encounter with the presence of God. It reveals the holiness of the moment at hand.

St John of the Cross spoke of this when he taught that even in between our prayer of passive meditation, we are called to preserve a loving attentiveness to God with no desire to feel or understand any particular thing concerning God. It is just attending to the Lord, being present and returning to being present to Him whenever we become distracted.

It is realising that He is calling to us right now to be present, and it leads us to the idea that anything that calls our attention is, in some way, inviting us into receiving a word from the Lord.

Poetry Pause

The Paradox of Presence

Here I am Lord;
I am a passing shadow
I am a breath on the edge of being
I am a body of dust and ashes

I am a child of earth
I am from nothing
I am only ever almost
I am a ripple in the pool of life
I am a whisper in the silence
I am lost in time
I am unfulfilled yearning
I am a distorted reflection
I am delusion
I am desire
I am for now
And yet,
Here I am Lord;
I am made in your image
I am growing into your likeness
I am an idea in the Divine mind
I am called forth from nothingness
I am an exhalation of love
I am a child of God
I am an eternal soul
I am a word spoken by the Word
I am the temple of the Divine
I am from Being itself
I am called by name
I am held in being by Love
I am interpenetrated by light
I am sustained by pure attention
I am healed by Divine Compassion
I am redeemed by mercy

times of designated formal sitting practice, everything becomes practice – every act, every motion of our being becomes sacred, and a sense of oneness with Divine Love is maintained throughout the day.

Becoming Whole and Holy through Meditation

We need to remember that the word 'holy' and the word 'holistic' have similar meanings. Holistic comes from the Greek word *holos* and means 'balanced'. Holy in English comes from the old English *halig*, which became *hal*, which meant healthy, uninjured and whole.

A holy person is then both whole and balanced, someone who has found peace and stability in the presence of the Divine so that their life slowly transforms. They have entered a place of centred equanimity and peace. The surface of their lives may be stormy, as are the lives of most people, but, in their hearts, they are at peace and, in their souls, the storms are calmed as they love from the awareness of the presence of God.

People living from this attitude are now in, or are at least working towards, a right relationship with the Divine, with themselves, with others and even with the cosmos.

This is what it is to live a peaceful, holy life. A balanced life, an integrated life, even a holistic life can grow from these practices. This person lives aware of

Divine Presence in the present moment, so far as this is possible, and so holiness, wholeness and balance are maintained throughout the day.

One of the primary attitude adjusters we can practise in this part of our meditative training is to return to the remembrance that there is never a moment when we are outside the Divine Presence.

We see this taught in that beautiful Psalm 139: 'If I go up to the heavens, You are there; if I make my bed in the depths, You are there. If I rise on the wings of the dawn and dwell on the far side of the sea, even there Your hand will guide me, Your right hand will hold me fast.'

The great mystic and doctor of the Church St Catherine of Siena, when speaking of the closeness of God's presence in her famous work the *Dialogue,* puts it this way: 'The soul is in God and God is in the soul, just as the fish is in the sea and the sea is in the fish.'

We are that close, we are held in being by the attention of Divine Love and becoming aware of that love moment by moment.

This is such an important teaching, and one that we often fail to understand when we are still thinking in a non-meditative way of time and space.

When I used to teach seminarians and youth ministers, I always had to tell them to be very careful if they thought they were 'bringing God' into any place or to any person. 'Your job,' I would remind them, as my teachers had reminded me, 'is not to bring God anywhere. Your job is to meet God where you are in the people and situations you find yourself with and then in your own heart and life too.

This is so important because it reminds us that, in all of our difficult circumstances, there is never a space that we enter into – even if it is an anxious space, a stressful space, a worried space, a broken space or even a sinful space – that God isn't already in. God is already there waiting for us. God is already there loving us and inviting us, in that moment, to grow in our awareness, to love more deeply or, in the case of selfishness and sin, to repent and come home to His loving presence.

St Teresa of Ávila said the greatest mistake most beginners to meditation make is to think that when they are good enough, God will show up! She said they are like the person who spends all day looking at the window, waiting for the visitor, and the visitor is already sitting in the chair behind them.

The problem for so many of us is that, where love is concerned, we have been taught from a very early age to think that we will be loved only when we are good enough – so the better we become, the more we will be loved.

While this might be true at a human level – even if it's not the best way to love or be loved – it is certainly not true with God. In your darkest moment of sin and in your most sanctified and holy moment, God loves you to exactly the same degree. God may not love the 'how' you are living, but God always loves the 'who' that is living that life.

So many of us find this very hard to comprehend because it's not the way we deal with our fellow humans, and so we posit a Creator who is kind of just waiting to catch us out, rather than the God who Jesus reveals as the One who is a communion of love.

When we come to know God as the One who is love we are able to recognise that there is nothing outside of this loving embrace, so there is nothing within us that can't become a path to the holy experience of love if given to the transforming power of His love and grace.

When we realise this within our meditation, this gives us a contemplative vision of our own life (and the life of all people of all times and places), as the beloved of God to whom is made known the fullness of Divine Love in Christ.

This is where we begin to experience God's love, peace, joy and abundance in a moment-to-moment way.

Practice: The Presence in the Present

Let's take a moment to begin to practise being aware of God in the present moment.

Find a comfortable seat in a quiet space, place your

feet flat on the floor and your back comfortably straight, take a moment to settle yourself and simply pause.

Adjust your body if you need so that you are in a comfortable but alert position that enables your breathing to move gently and your back to remain straight.

Try to ensure that your feet are flat on the ground and your hands are resting palm upwards on your lap.

Gently begin to notice how you are in this moment.

Check in with your body and notice any sensation that moves across your bodily awareness.

If you need to adjust your position, do so.

Allow your feet to rest secure on the ground and your back to relax against the chair.

Allow the chair to carry your weight.

Starting with the soles of your feet slowly move up the body, noticing any particular sensation that may be present.

If there are any that draw your attention simply mentally mark these for yourself by naming them, and then move on.

When you reach the crown of your head, pause for a moment.

Now check in with your emotions, with your feelings.

How are you feeling in this moment?

However you are you are.

Accept the reality of your feelings and do not try and change them.

If there are struggles or difficulties in your life, do not be afraid to recall them.

Notice any tightening in your body or emotional movement as you recall them.

For now, though, simply notice these things but do not become attached to them.

Now begin to move your awareness to your breath.

Do not change your breathing in any way, just notice your breath.

Feel the coolness of the air as it enters your body and the warmth of the air as it leaves your body.

If you can, try and follow the path of your breath from the moment it enters your body to the moment it leaves your body.

After a few moments of this, try to notice the point where the in-breath becomes the out-breath and where the out-breath becomes the in-breath.

As you focus on that point, allow your body to relax. Let your legs become heavy, solid and grounded, with your back resting securely against the chair.

As you rest in the awareness of your breath and of the midpoint in the cycle of your breath, where in becomes out and where out becomes in, follow that point to the centre of your being to a place of perfect peace and perfect rest.

Rest in that place, and as you rest in that place relax and become still.

Listening to the words of scripture that follow, allow them to resound in your mind, all the while simply breathing in and breathing out.

Be still and know that I am God.

Be still and know that I am God.

Be still and know that I am.

Be still and know that I am.

Be still and know

Be still and know

Be still

Be still

Be

Be

For a moment rest in the awareness of the presence of God.

Rest in the stillness at the centre of your being.

Rest in the presence of God, who knows you and loves you infinitely and unconditionally.

Take a few moments anchored in your breath, anchored in the knowledge that you rest in the presence of God.

If you feel distracted, simply notice the distraction and return to your breath.

Occasionally, you may like to repeat inwardly the line of scripture, 'Be still and know.'

After a few moments, allow your awareness to move

beyond your breath to the pressure of the floor against your feet and the chair against your back.

Gently, begin to notice the sounds around you.

Before you return to ordinary awareness, take a moment to give thanks in your own words.

Chapter 6

Meaning and Purpose

To grow in this practice and really see its transforming effect in our lives we must start with the two primary orienting principles of human life – meaning and purpose – and then see how the practice of the four inner directions of meditation helps us to live those orienting principles in a balanced and holistic manner.

One way of meditatively describing our human life is to see it as unfolding along two great axes of human life: meaning and purpose.

Let me explain.

Imagine your life from birth to death as a horizontal line, as a chronological line with the beginning known but the ending at some unknown point in the future (like the number lines we used to plot out in primary school). We can use this line to illustrate the axis of purpose – of human activity laid out in time. Each year, each day, each moment of the day is a point on that line. We can divide it into smaller and smaller increments of time and activities almost ad infinitum.

But this isn't the whole picture.

There is another more important axis in our life. The axis of meaning. This vertical axis reveals the depth to our existence, it is the eternal part of our lives, the life of our soul, as it were.

What we find, of course, when we plot the latter axis over the former is that that vertical axis – the one of meaning – intersects the horizontal line of our life not just once but in every single succeeding present moment (an infinity of present moment points upon the life line, in fact), but only if we attend to it. Only if we apply our mindfulness to it.

Of course, what we discover in our Christian contemplative tradition as it views these two axes is human reality is revealed as a being who dwells in every succeeding moment in both time and eternity, in both what the old monks called *chronos* (chronological time) and contemplatively in what they called *kairos* (the eternal present moment of God's saving love in Christ made present through the incarnation).

So, in our meditative view of life, purpose is that horizontal axis – the day-to-day activity of life that, by itself, doesn't have a huge amount of meaning until we bring in the awareness of the eternal dimension that transcends purpose and brings us into the depth of the vertical axis.

This is entering the present moment at a profoundly deep level, as a place of encounter with the ultimate dimension of reality that in the Christian tradition we speak of as Divine Presence.

Living from our practice of meditation means always remembering that it is meaning that gives us our purpose, and not our purpose (however good it may be) that gives us our meaning.

In fact, one of the great crises in the world today that is addressed by the rebalancing of the human through meditative practice is that we've trained whole generations of people for purpose, but we haven't trained them for meaning.

In other words, we have trained people to be busy (busyness is one of the great storms of current life, remember) to the point that they do not have time to reflect on the inner meaning or narrative of vocation in their life. If we cannot connect to even the question of meaning, of having a life that is coherent with transcendent principles that humanity has always thought of as important (the pursuit of the true, the beautiful and the good, for example), then no matter how successful we are in matters of purposeful activity, we will find an inner emptiness that no level of success will ever fill. I think of those young men and women that I used to meet when I was a college chaplain and they would have done three, four or five years of undergrad and post-grad study for a particular profession and towards the end they would sit in front of me and they would say, 'I don't want to be this.'

They would say how they had realised that they didn't want to be an architect or a doctor or whatever. But they were only coming to this awareness after all their years of study because, up until that point, they had been kept so busy that they didn't have time for that moment of reflection to become aware of how they truly felt about their life journey. Without a reflective space that enabled them to touch meaning, they had become lost in their own lives. Meditative practice protects that reflective space, exercises its muscles and trains a person to seek meaning before purpose, indeed to allow their search for meaning to inform the kind of purposeful activity they want to fill their lives with.

So as someone who practises meditation, we are choosing to dwell as much as we can – consciously each day and in each moment – in the centre of the cross, that intersection between these two axes, in the present moment.

This intersection is the point of true reality: this is the place where the fullness of human life happens. It is the place of the Now and so is also the only place of true choice and freedom. This is the place of transcendence and depth, the place where God is encountered. It is the place of the present moment hallowed and deepened by mindful attention and so, when we are consciously in the present moment, we are at one at the same time, encountering the Divine and our own life in their proper relationship, in the shalom, the peace, that enables us to be the icon of the Divine in the world, while also discovering the present moment as place of the revelation of Divine Presence.

Where Every Bush Is Burning

One of the most important revelations of God that is described in the scriptures, and that gives us a deep insight into our entire meditative tradition, is that wonderful story of Moses before the burning bush where he receives the revelation of the Divine Name as Yahweh, which literally translates as the 'I AM'. You can find it all to read for yourself in chapter three of the Book of Exodus.

Most importantly for our work here, the mystical interpretation of that name down the ages is one recognised by many of our Jewish brothers and sisters as well as the meditative Christian tradition as God revealing himself as 'the Now', as in fact the essence of the present moment, or at least as the eternal ultimate transcendent ground of the Now as we experience it in time. In our meditation, Divine Love is encountered as the transcendent present and the present moment may be encountered as a manifestation of the Divine.

This is why so many of the mystics and teachers of

meditation will go so far as to speak of the 'sacrament of the present moment'. Meaning that, like the seven great sacraments of the Church, that are visible signs of invisible graces, we may say that the present moment itself, as we encounter it in God, has a sacramental character whereby, when we receive it meditatively and prayerfully, it opens us up to the ongoing revelation of God's love and providential action in the world and bestows an encounter with the meaning axis of our lives. Spiritual teachers, such as Francis de Sales, Faustina, Thérèse of Lisieux, Lawrence of the Resurrection and many, many others, have taught the importance of this realisation for the person who wishes to grow in the practice of meditation.

And so, in this revelation as described in Exodus chapter three, we see the invisible becomes visible in God breathing all things into existence and holding them in existence. So, in loving connection to the present moment as it arises from God, we are connected to all of the past, present and future in one great communion of love, one great field of Divine Love.

Now, of course, it's easy to say to someone to simply rest in the present moment and all will be fine. As we saw earlier there is much being made of the 'present moment' and even the quality of mindfulness of the present or simple awareness as a positive element of psychological health that can help people who are suffering from anxiety and depression.

To just be in the present, well that's great, and,

psychologically, it can be helpful as a practice. But for Christians, pursuing the meditative way, it's important for us to know what we're talking about when we speak of practising 'abiding in the present moment' or 'dwelling in the sacrament of the present moment'. We mean that, in the present moment, we become aware that like Moses we are standing in the fire of the burning bush. That, in the present moment, we are on holy ground! But we will only perceive this if we 'take off our sandals' – in other words, if we have the humility to slow down, purify our senses through cultivating meditative attention and waiting on the inner revelation of Divine Love. In other words, to become still so that we may know!

When this happens we begin to see things as they actually are. To the one dwelling in meditation, every 'bush' (every place and every moment) is aflame with the glory of God, every person is on fire constantly with the light of Divine Love, but we don't see it because most of the time we are not in the present moment with God. We are lost in travelling mentally through time, lost in the anxiety storms or busyness storms of our lives or stuck on the horizontal axis of purpose alone – but if we could see things as they actually are, then we would see that flame, that light, constantly. We would then be dwelling at the sacred cross-point of meaning and purpose.

Poetry Pause

I Am

Until the I am
rests fully within the I Am
I am not what I am.
Until the I am
surrenders its I to the I Am
it cannot know itself fully or truly as I.
Until the I am is detached
from all that it believes it possesses
it cannot be aware that it is possessed
by the
I Am.
Until the I am empties itself
of all it believes it is
it cannot be filled by the truth
of who it is in the I Am.
Until the I am is silenced at its heart
the I Am cannot be heard.
Until the I am is stilled
it will not know the I Am as
the still-source of all movement.
Until the I am yearns not
for the past and the future
it will not rest fully within
the Now of the
I Am.

Until the I am loves without
being afraid of losing the beloved
it will not know the I Am is
LOVE.

The Exodus revelation story then invites us into the knowing of the God who is holding all things in being, and who IS being itself.

So, the present moment becomes the place of meditative encounter. It becomes the place of the burning bush, the place where the inner sun is rising. When the ancient Jewish sages reflected on this lovely moment of the burning bush, they referred to God as revealing himself as *Hamakom* (the place), for if all things exist in and through God then the Divine Presence is the only place there is. There is no place outside *Hamakom*, outside the place, for you cannot be outside of Divine Presence.

Here are some practices of meaning and purpose.

Practice 1: Drawing the Axes of Meaning and Purpose

Take a moment to settle yourself where you have a table, a notebook or blank paper and some writing or drawing tools.

Leave the materials on the table in front of you.

Find a comfortable seat in a quiet space, place your

feet flat on the floor and your back comfortably straight, take a moment to settle yourself and simply pause.

Become aware of the ebb and flow of your breath.

Feel the movement of the breath in your body as it rises and falls.

Feel the movement of the breath as your anchor to the present moment.

Try and notice the coolness of the breath as it enters your body.

Try and notice the warmth of the breath as it leaves your body.

After observing the breath for three cycles of in and out breathing, go back in your memory to the moment you woke this morning and ask yourself how you woke.

Try and see yourself waking up in your mind's eye. Ask yourself:

- Did you wake to meaning or purpose?

- Did you wake to worry, anxiety or a list of things you had to do later in the day, or thoughts about the future or past?

Now draw the horizontal timeline of purpose from yesterday, from the moment you got up to the moment you went to bed.

Along the timeline fill in any important points where events happened.

Look at the timeline.
Ask yourself:

- In those moments was I aware?

- In those moments was I connected to meaning?

- In those moments was I using my reflective capacity?

(If the answer to these questions is negative, please do not feel bad or blame yourself. Remember, this exercise is only about noting habitual patterns of distraction from meaning so that we can begin to remedy this.)

Now begin to intersect the moments listed on your timeline with the vertical axis of meaning and ask yourself, 'How would I have acted differently if I had been dwelling in meditative awareness when these things happened?'

Try and see in your mind's eye the differences that may have been manifest in you or in the situation had you been fully present to it.

You may like to note for yourself any insights that arise so as to carry them forward.

When finished, lay down your writing materials and return to just being with the breath in the present moment for three cycles of in- and out-breath.

At the end you may like to offer a prayer or thought of gratitude for any of the insights you have received.

Practice 2: Finding Moments of Meaning and Purpose in Life

In order to do this practice well it can help to have pen and paper or a journal to hand.

Find a comfortable seat in a quiet space, place your feet flat on the floor and your back comfortably straight, take a moment to settle yourself and simply pause.

Choose to be aware of your breath.

Gently and inwardly, invoke the presence of God, recognising that at all times He is already present to us, but we are tuning in to Him.

At this point take three cycles of in-breath and out-breath to relax the body and to draw your focus to the present moment.

As you breathe, you may like to unite your prayer word or *versiculum*.

A way of praying this particular moment with reference to the scripture you have just looked at is to allow the divine name Yahweh to be your prayer word.

Breathe in on the first syllable, Yah.

Breathe out on the second syllable, -weh.

Yah-weh.

Yah-weh.

Yah-weh.

After some time in stillness and being present to the breath and the word, take a moment to draw a horizontal line on your page or in your journal.

Let this represent your chronological life story from your birth until today.

So far as you can, indicate along the line important moments to your spiritual journey, perhaps indicating them by your age or by symbol or simply by naming them.

Now draw a vertical line through each of these moments and recognise the intersection of meaning and purpose in your life during those sacred events.

Notice how engaging with the meaning of these moments had set a purposeful direction to subsequent activity.

As time goes on, you can return to this graph and fill in more events of meaning and of purpose as you remember them, thus beginning to discover the inter-play of these two axes in your past to discern their presence more readily in the present.

After a few moments contemplating your drawing, lay down your pen and return to your breath and the word for at least three cycles.

Before leaving your meditation make the resolution to dwell more often in the sacredness of the present moment.

Before you conclude, take a moment to give thanks for the events you have recorded as wisdom moments for yourself.

Fullness and Emptiness

Moving more deeply into this understanding that the balance of meaning and purpose bestow the meditative view that the Divine Presence is 'the place' and that nothing that exists is outside of Divine Presence, we may be led by the early mystics in Judaism and the early Monastic Fathers and Mothers to say that we may at different times encounter this place of Divine Presence in different ways, sometimes in a *via positiva,* where there are those who will come to know God through talking, through the intellect and through the imagination. This is the way of positive statement and discursive meditation. But there are those who will know God through simply being present to Him in a loving gaze without seeking necessarily to understand via the intellect. This is the *via negativa* of Christian mysticism, where the meditator dwells in God as the ultimate mystery and the transcendent ground of our and all being.

I remember some years ago, I was chatting with a Buddhist monk. We were teaching workshops at a kind of 'traditions-in-dialogue' gathering and he saw much commonality in our traditions, in the sense that the Buddha taught that if God exists, then that God would be so far beyond our understanding as human beings that it would be better for us to say nothing about that God and wait for that God to speak – so, he said, as Buddhists we say nothing about God and instead speak of the Ultimate and of Emptiness. 'But,' he said, 'you believe God spoke! And that is the essential difference.'

We believe that God 'spoke', and that God can speak in our emptiness just as much as in our fullness and that, though we may experience emptiness, it is an emptiness without absence, a Divine spaciousness that still bestows ultimate meaning even if that is utterly transcendent. God is with us, always inviting us into an ever deeper and more transformative relationship.

Poetry Pause

Home

What if I told you
that the
emptiness
you feel
is not absence
but a boundless
presence.
Would you know
you were in a room
at all
if it was so vast
you could not
sense

the floor,
the ceiling,
the walls?
Yet,
you were made
for such
spaciousness
as your true
home.
What if I told you
that the darkness
you fear to enter
is only
a luminosity so bright
you are blinded
by its intensity,
as prisoners stumble
blinking into
the first dawn
of freedom.
Yet you were made
for such light
as your true
home.
What if I told you
that the
stillness
you find so
difficult

to even touch
for a moment
is already
an ocean
of dynamic peace
within you
and around you
through which you
dance
each day,
and from which
your very being
arises.
Yet you were made
for such stillness
as your true
home.
Emptiness
without absence.
Bright darkness.
Stillness dancing.
All arising from love.
And love is
home.

Chapter 7

The Four Inner Directions – Intention, Attention, Compassion and Wisdom

Through our meditation practice, we can come to dwell in the present moment as the place of Divine Presence and Love, and we see that the present moment, when attended to mindfully via the practice of meditation, is revealed as the place of intersection between our daily purpose and our eternal meaning. We will want to ensure that we try and stay oriented towards encountering that meaning in the present moment even when consumed by purpose.

So how do we do this?

A way of ensuring that this orientation towards living deeply in the present moment happens is to work with those meditative practices the tradition hands down. These may be seen as arising from the four 'inner directions' of meditation: intention, attention, compassion and wisdom.

These directions provide both a map and a list of practices by which we can place ourselves in the present moment and enable us to see what directions we need to move in to develop a more contemplative presence in our lives. These four directions of meditative practice become reference points to ensure we hold ourselves aware at the level of inner meaning. We can begin to use them as an inner compass to direct and deepen our practice.

I remember speaking to a group of young people just on the cusp of leaving secondary school. Their great fear was, in their own words, that they would 'get lost' in their own lives.

I think we can each become lost in our own life at times. The storms of anxiety, fast-paced living, stress and busyness can disorientate us somewhat. But the more we bring ourselves into the deep awareness that our own individual story is a part of the infinitely greater story of Divine Love, the more we become clear that we can never get lost in our own life again.

The four directions of meditation do this job for the practitioner. They provide us with a mechanism to establish balance in our mindfulness and meditative practices, while ensuring that our meditation does not fall into a kind of quietism sometimes recognised today with the phrase 'spiritual bypassing' – a temptation to use our practice as a way to avoid things like community effort, social and personal responsibility, hard work and even sometimes the practice itself.

There is a wonderful story from the Desert Fathers that illustrates this temptation of meditation as an avoidance of service and compassion.

A young monk went to his Abba and said that he was going to give up all his manual work and just devote himself completely to meditation.

The Abba smiled and said, 'OK, why not go and try it for a while.'

So, the monk went to a cell on the outskirts of the monastery and spent the morning in practice. At lunch-time, the bell rang and the brothers gathered in the refectory. The young monk stayed in his cell. He was now a man of meditative prayer, after all. But nobody brought him lunch.

So, he looked out the window . . . still nobody was coming. He heard the bell in the distance and saw the brothers leaving the refectory and going back to work. Nobody had come to get him. *They must have forgotten about me*, he thinks. He forgave them – after all, he was now a man of prayer.

But the next day came and, again, nobody brought him food. The day after that came, and the day after. Now, he could no longer meditate – his mind was solely taken up with how hungry he was. He was beginning to feel weak. Finally, he left his cell and went to the monastery. He knocked on the Abba's door and with some anger said, 'Abba, I'm up there doing the work of the angels and nobody brought me any food!'

The Abba looked at him with love and replied, 'But, brother, angels don't eat!'

The young monk returned to the work of the community that very moment.

So, we need to ensure that our practice has balance!

The consideration of the four inner directions of meditation gives us this beautiful balance as they are transformative of both the inner and the outer personal reality and give lenses by which we may judge our practice and its ongoing effect in our lives. In the Christian tradition of meditation, we always remember our need to be transforming on both levels at all times, even when we live in a world that often only values transformation at the outer level.

There was a series of adverts for cosmetics in Ireland some years ago, the whole maxim of which was: 'If you want to feel good on the inside, you've got to look good on the outside!' This is a complete reversal of the entire spiritual wisdom of humanity. We need our compass for the journey in order to ensure our balance.

So what do these inner directions entail?

The four inner directions of meditation – intention, attention, compassion and wisdom – allow us to enter into a balanced meditative life that provides us with inner equanimity even while enduring the storms of everyday life. As these directions are sought out, travelled and practised the meditator will find their inner life deepening, their awareness growing; the quality of being mindful begins to be applied to all aspects of life and not just to times of formal meditation practice and so real transformation is seen. These 'inner directions' give a meditative lens through which all of life may be viewed and so lend a sense of perspective that allows us to see the storms as temporary (no matter how long they may last), as having no effect on our essential worth or being.

The first two of the directions – intention and attention – are the core practices of a meditative life, while the second two – compassion and wisdom – are the fruits of meditative practice.

All four of the directions require us to base ourselves in simple mindfulness practice as a beginning. It is compassion that stretches out from us to others and offers the transformation of our relational life, wisdom is that fruit of practice that transcends the self within, but without intention and attention, and without the building of mindful awareness, compassion and wisdom are not generated consistently.

The meditator may be said to sit in the middle of these four inner paths, at the nexus point, if you will, between those four directions. We can check in on ourselves with them by asking:

What is my intention in this moment?

Where is my attention in this moment?

Does my practice result in compassion in this moment?

Does my practice result in wisdom in this moment?

This gentle inner questioning enables us to be aware of how our practice is going and what needs to be attended to for us to reach new depths of equanimity in response to the storms of life.

It should be also understood that each of the four directions will have some of the elements of the other three in them while, at different times, they will centre themselves on one over the others.

Let us look at them individually and at the practices that go with them.

INTENTION

Intention practices were also known in the tradition as the 'practices of consecration'. Today, we often think of consecration in very limited ways. We see consecration as giving ourselves or things to God. Monastic life is often called 'consecrated life', for example.

But there is another meaning to that word, consecration – coming from its roots, *con sacris*, to be with that which is sacred. So, if I am living with or even simply practising with intention, then I may see myself as stepping into a sacred place as I live the practices of consecration.

Intention, then, seeks to encounter the heart, the hidden room of the soul.

As we will see, in living intentionally, we are not living from our physical appetites (which often consume us) and we are not living from our egoic desires (which can burn us up and give us a sense of unreality) and we are not living from our worries or our anxieties or family patterns. Thus, the storms of life are not just calmed, but we are removed from the possibility of even generating the storms.

Even with the best of intention (if you'll pardon the pun!), we can only truly live intentionally on a moment-by-moment basis. We all know what it's like, don't we? We get up in the morning and we have the intention to live with awareness, with a deeper, more meditative consciousness. We are clear that we will not get caught up in the inner stormy weather of our mind and heart. We rise and say to ourselves, 'Today, I shall begin. I will live with awareness all day!' So we start the day well, with a good general intention.

But then we meet somebody who distracts us, or raises old patterns in us, or we look at ourselves in the mirror and get lost in judgement or comparison – and off we go into the storms again and our focus is lost. We simply have to live with the inevitability of distraction and temptation, which will pull us from this fundamental intention towards inner awareness in the present moment. But, and here's the secret, that is actually okay.

If you want to keep nurturing an intentional life then, above all else, you shouldn't add anxiety about distractions into the mix of your meditation. If you do, then all you've done is distract yourself from the distraction – and the new distraction provides a second layer, which now places us two steps away from our desired intentional reality.

Instead, we simply recognise distractions when they arise as distractions, and then we let them go without considering or grasping them. When you let them go, you simply renew your intention to be present each time. This is the first step in living with intention and like all first steps it influences the rest of the journey greatly.

Intentional practices are the initial practices that help you to clear the tangled ground of your mind for the cultivation of deep meditation. After all, if you want to have a beautiful garden, the first thing you have to do is clear the ground, and only then will you choose what will go into that garden.

Intention clears the ground in a way that enables even distractions and temptations to reveal themselves as positive tools that teach us where our vulnerabilities lie and which areas of our life are in need of grace.

Thus, the garden is transformed, and everything finds its appropriate place in the psyche.

As the great Christian mystic and poet Robert Lax wrote in his poem 'Cultivation', our job is to transform the jungle into a garden without harming a single flower. It is an awareness that we are cultivating not to make our life sacred, but to grow in awareness of the sacredness existing within life already.

Our practice of intention comes from a single meditative truth: everything that is comes from Divine Love and so, in its original essence, it is good. Our intention is to seek out this original essence of a thing, of a being or of the moment at hand, and be with it fully.

What are the kinds of practice we can engage in to strengthen this primary direction of intention?

Many of them are well known, though over the years, as life has become ever more pressured and filled with storms of anxiety and stress, they have been forgotten, which is such a pity, especially as they are essential to meditative development.

Practice 1: The Morning Offering

One of the most important practices – and its importance is something that most of the world's meditative traditions are in agreement on – is the consecration of our first moment of wakefulness in the morning, our first moment of conscious awareness, by choosing to live the day with a clear intention. In the Christian monastic tradition we use this practice as a way of entering Divine Presence and holding an intention to remain united consciously to Divine Love throughout the day.

Now, how do you usually wake up?

Are you dragged unwilling out of sleep? Is it: *Oh no, here we go again!* Is it a case of reaching for the phone immediately in order to catch up on all the bad news quickly or to see what you've missed during the night? Feeding all of your anxieties and stresses and entering into that inner storm of the distracted again?

As one old priest I knew used to tell me, our fundamental way of orienting the day may simply come down to the choice as to whether on waking we say, 'Good morning, God, or good God it's morning!' The former is the one we are aiming for because if we situate ourselves in a place of inner space, stillness, meditation and peace in those first seconds of our day, we are setting a direction – an intention – for the rest of the day that is very powerful and that will put us on the meditative path immediately.

To begin intentionally and with mindful awareness is to set a course for the day that is positive, gentle and meaningful – and from which comes a right-ordering of our purpose of that day towards inner meaning.

In order to shape this moment, and to train your mind and heart into it becoming a core practice of your life, we can use the ancient practice of the 'morning offering'. There are many formal 'acts of morning offering' that can be made. But you may simply like to stabilise yourself in a moment of deep stillness as soon as you consciously can. Switch off the alarm and switch on your intention! It can be very helpful to bring the body into this too as a way of ensuring we don't fall back asleep or lose touch with our awareness of the day as a new beginning. Try the following practice for a few days and then make it your own.

As soon as the alarm rings, switch it off and get out of bed.

Find a comfortable seat in a quiet space, place your feet flat on the floor and your back comfortably straight, take a moment to settle yourself and simply pause.

Sit in quiet comfort for a few moments.

Re acquaint yourself with the rhythm of your breath.

Be with the ebb and flow of in-breath and out-breath.

If it helps you to focus on the breath place one hand on your abdomen, and one on your chest and be with the sensations of your breathing for a few moments.

When you feel like you have settled you can say inwardly, or out loud if you are comfortable to do so:

A new day begins.

I give thanks I am here to see it.

I enter this day intentionally and with awareness.

I will try to return to this intention from time to time throughout the day.

I choose to be awake.

I choose to learn.

I choose to love.

I will attend to the present moment.

I will allow the past to be the past.

I will allow the future to be the future.

I will attend to the present moment.

Then return to the breath for three cycles of in-breath and out-breath and then move to the next task of the day. You can check in with yourself throughout the day to see if you are still in touch with your original intention and if necessary recalibrate.

If you are combining this moment of primary intention with prayer then you may like to use some of the traditional formulas of Morning Offerings. Two of the best known are given below.

Firstly the simple child's one:

'Oh my God, you love me,
You're with me night and day,
I want to love you always,
In all I do and say,
I'll try to please you Father,
Bless me through the day.
Amen.'

Or the older adult version:

'O Jesus, through the Immaculate Heart of Mary, I offer You my prayers, works, joys, and sufferings of this day in union with the Holy Sacrifice of the mass throughout the world. I offer them for all the intentions of Your Sacred Heart: the salvation of souls, reparation for sin, and the reunion of all Christians.'

There are many, many other ways of making such an intentional offering, of course, but they all boil down to a moment of placing ourselves intentionally and deliberately in the presence of deeper reality and offering all that we are, have and do in co-operation with the action of Divine Love in our lives and in the world.

The purpose then of this morning offering moment is to refine our intention. This opens up the other three directions as we begin our day with a promise to keep our attention centred on the present moment and to enjoy the benefits of working towards wisdom and compassion throughout the day.

These small practices of meditative prayer to set intention were often ritualised in the monastic life. In the Capuchin order, we had the tradition that when the bell rang to wake us up, we were to get straight out of the bed, kneel down and kiss the ground as an act of gratitude for another day to begin again in the presence of God. I've found it a very powerful practice myself, even though I've banged my head off the ground so many times from being half asleep in that moment!

A friend was telling me that they knew someone

who put the alarm under the bed so that, when it went off, they had to kneel down to make it to stop – their meditation begins right then with the thought, *Well, Lord, now that I'm here on my knees, I might as well start with meditation.*

So, we consecrate that moment, and it is a very special moment. But if you miss it, that's okay – hopefully you will get the chance to begin again tomorrow.

We don't beat ourselves up if we miss the moment. Instead, we dwell in the moment that we are actually in. The power of this moment is a grace-filled practice not to be underestimated. Saints have been made from the practice of the morning offering.

Practice 2: Resolution

The second practice of intention includes internal resolutions and promises.

When you make resolutions, you are declaring a definitive intention to live and practice in a particular way that is often transformative to your life, attitudes, habits and even your moral life. Resolutions are often characterised as somewhat negative. They can often be seen as about giving up things, but they can be truly positive if we are using them to make us more conscious of our inner life and our cultivation of a clear intention to grow spiritually.

Then make these inner statements to yourself:

I will walk with awareness on this journey to the local shop.

Or

I will wash this cup with generosity and gratitude for those I share my home with.

Or

I will listen to this person with patience and compassion.

Or

I will use my senses and breath to connect me to the present moment.

The gift of such inner resolutions is that they hone our intention to live with a quality of mindful awareness of the present moment, despite the storms of life all around us, and they also remove us from the grip of the unconscious repetition of patterned behaviour in an unthinking way.

Living these intentional statements consciously in the present moment invites us into the practice of constantly beginning again. This is, in a very real way, the essence of the spiritual tradition.

One of the great Desert Fathers was asked what the purpose of being in the desert was. He answered that it was to teach men and women to begin again. The art is beginning again and again and again. As reported by his biographer, Thomas of Celano, St Francis said to his brothers almost daily, 'Let us begin again for, up until now, we have done nothing.'

One of the most important resolutions we can make,

as a statement of inner intention, is to declare, 'Here I am. I begin again from here.'

In other words, you can't go back and change what has happened, but you can start from here and, with the wisdom you have gathered, set off in a new direction to create a new ending from this present moment.

To illustrate this a little more, I remember talking to a priest on a retreat. He was sixty-three when he was ordained, which would have been considered a 'late vocation'. He was a wonderful man and very joyful in his life when I met him, but he told me he was at one stage quite disconsolate, upset over all the time he had lived before he became a priest. He kept thinking about what he could have been doing with all that time.

This kept happening until he met a monk who said to him, 'But, Father, do you not realise that the Lord knew you would be ordained at sixty-three and was using everything before to enrich the kind of priest you'll be after sixty-three?'

You see, nothing is wasted, nothing. Everything we hand over with firm resolution and the intention to be present to Divine Love is transformed.

Nothing gets wasted and even our negative experiences, when considered gently and contemplatively, at least taught us how *not* to be.

So, we form our intention and then we strengthen it as we make our promises and resolutions to begin again. But if I 'break' these intentions, I consciously remember that this is just an invitation to begin again in grace.

Practice 3: Meditative Relationships

We may also consecrate our relationships and live them intentionally and with awareness by asking ourselves questions about the relationships we have with others. In our meditative sitting we can take some time to ask at least some of the questions below. It can be a good idea to journal the answers so as to be able to refer to them afterwards.

Find a comfortable seat in a quiet space, place your feet flat on the floor and your back comfortably straight, take a moment to settle yourself and simply pause.

Then ask yourself:

- Are people deepening my awareness or are they calling me away from my awareness?

- How can I be a point that deepens their awareness?

- Am I helping them live from the depth dimension?

- Am I a point in their life where they encounter Divine Love and compassion more deeply?

- Am I taking them away from their relationship with Divine Love?

To ask these questions with deep intention is to see transformation occur where we can then resolve to begin again.

Practice 4: Asceticism and Awareness

In the Christian tradition, the practice of meditation was always seen to have an ascetical character to it. It takes sacrifice to develop meditatively. Today, the word sacrifice is not very fashionable, we all tremble at the thought of it somewhat, but this is often because we don't understand it fully in the context of intentionality.

From the times of the Desert Fathers, the tradition was very clear that the practice of sacrifice can help to hone intentionality and strengthen our attentiveness. When we look at these practices in this way, they present a more positive experience.

Sacrifice is where intention becomes action. It comes from the words 'to make sacred' in Latin. Meditatively, this primarily means gifting something to God that is of value. This does not need to be seen as a negative thing, like the way a child sees giving up sweets for Lent. Rather, this is part of our practice of the consecration of time, space and our person to Divine Presence by living in an intentional way.

What is important to understand with these practices is the recognition that, when offered lovingly and with clear intention, they deepen our sensitivity and awareness by cleansing our senses so often overwhelmed by the storms of media, noise and overconsumption, and give them space to recover their original sensitivity.

So, what do we sacrifice as part of our practice?

Find a comfortable seat in a quiet space, place your feet flat on the floor and your back comfortably straight, take a moment to settle yourself and simply pause.

Then, slowly start to think about sacrifice and how it relates to the practice of meditation and awareness.

The primary sacrifice is, of course, the time we devote to meditation. When we make the intention to meditate, that is a good thing in and of itself. But, of course, we want to carry the intention onwards into the actual practice of attentive presence. Intention alone is not enough.

While there are great traditional practices of spiritual sacrifice like pilgrimage or fasting, or like giving up meat on Fridays and abstaining from sugar or alcohol during Lent, it's important to find sacrifices that mean something to your particular context.

For example, some people offer a spiritual fast on bread and water twice a week, and all of the great religions have seasons of fasting and deeper practice, but while that is great in itself, fasting from television or fasting from your phone or from gossip might be much more of a sacrifice for you and, therefore, more deeply transformative over time.

Practice 5: Discerning the Sacrifice

Find a comfortable seat in a quiet space, place your feet flat on the floor and your back comfortably straight, take a moment to settle yourself and simply pause.

You may like to connect with your breath as your anchor in practice once again.

Watch the ebb and flow of the breath for a little while.

Follow the path of the breath as it fills your lungs and then as it is returned to the air.

Reconnect with your morning intention to dwell with awareness in Divine Presence in the present moment.

Ask yourself: 'What has led me away from that intention today so far?'

Then with a calm heart simply look back over the day so far and watch what has moved your mind away from its original intention to be present.

Ask yourself: 'What do I need to do less of, or more of, in order to hold more fully to my intention?'

Answer your question gently and truthfully.

Make a resolution to change something based on your review, all the while breathing in and breathing out gently.

Then when the review comes to an end return to an awareness only of the breath for three cycles of in-breath and out-breath.

End with a little moment of gratitude for the awareness you have received.

Practice 6: Positive Examination of Conscience

Intentional awareness is not just about listing our failures, a negative examination of conscience as it were. So often, our examination of our own self is only about if or how we failed or got something wrong. While that is important, of course, we also need to have the other side present in these moments, to understand where the grace of God was present in our day.

Find a comfortable seat in a quiet space, place your feet flat on the floor and your back comfortably straight, take a moment to settle yourself and simply pause.

Then ask yourself:

- Where was I aware of Divine Presence in my brother or my sister?

- Where did I have a moment of awareness of Divine Love or Presence and then give thanks for that?

In time, this growing mindful awareness born of intentionality enables us to be aware of the good that is actually there in all lives all of the time; it is a fundamental goodness that the storms of our habits, distractions and worries prevent us from noticing.

For the Christian, when practised in this way, this positive intentionality enables us to live from a balanced understanding of ourselves as fundamentally the beloved of God, and this, in turn, enables every moment and movement of our being to have the potential to be holy and sacred, if we attend to it in the right way and, with discernment, make the right choices according to our primary intention. When we come to live this way, then even when we name the brokenness of our lives and become aware of its effects, we realise that we are simply called to surrender them to God and to take whatever action is needed to move our lives back to alignment with our intention.

Intentionality and Unknowing

In that late medieval manual of Christian meditative practice known as *The Cloud of Unknowing*, the author (probably an English Carthusian monk) spoke of the importance of forming a deliberate and clear intention to cling to Divine Presence in the present moment as the primary step for all further development in meditation.

This cultivation of what that author called the 'naked intent' – a deliberate act of intentionality, via the will, to be present to the Divine while letting go of all images and concepts – is the very start of the practice of contemplative awareness and leads to the other directions. Unfortunately, nowadays we are so distracted by the storms of anxiety and the constant bombardment of our senses by countless images and sounds we cannot begin here anymore and must first develop the quality of mindful awareness as we have seen already.

However, having developed our mindful practice we can then move onto developing intention, this naked intent towards the Divine or ultimate meaning. Without it, we cannot hone inner attention and, as we will see, it is only with the movement to inner attention that we begin to develop an inner equanimity of spirit that enables us to dwell in centred awareness beyond the reach of the storms of distraction and anxiety.

So, now that we know the necessity of cultivating that clear 'naked intent' towards Divine Love, that intentionality of life that leads us to the consecration of time, space and personhood towards transcendent encounter, let us move on to the heart of the practice, becoming consciously present to the Divine in the present moment, the second direction, the art of inner attention.

ATTENTION

Attention – the conscious awareness of the moment – was seen by the early monastics as an energy of the soul that lights the goal to which they were intending. Christ illumines this truth for us in the gospel when He says: 'Where your treasure is, there also is your heart' (Mt 6:21).

When we see what the heart, the conscious centre of the person, attends to, there we can see the goal of our very being revealed. In other words, what we focus our attention on, that is where we will be really present, that is who we really are.

So, to live meditatively, you must ask yourself:

- What takes up my heart (my centre)?

- What takes up my attention?

Attentiveness, both inward of the thoughts arising and outward of the present moment as it arises, was seen as absolutely necessary for meditative practice because it began the taming of the egoic or animal soul, the desiring part of the soul that seeks the selfish fulfilment of its own desires at the expense of the other.

For the Christian, this fostering of inner attention is a way of building or discerning the Kingdom of God within us. But its importance was seen in every meditative tradition, and it is at the core of every meditative practice as the first, most necessary and primary step towards contemplative union with the Divine or the transcendent dimension of reality.

This skill of attention is different to simple mindfulness, though it is descended from it. The direction of attention is a gathering of our mindfulness from a simple dwelling in a more sensitive field of awareness into a highly focused use of the faculty of attention.

Without cultivating attention, we simply do not proceed further along the path.

The twentieth-century monk and mystic Thomas Merton said in *Love and Living* that humanity in his day was so distracted that we were living in a state of constant semi-attention.

Goodness knows what he would think of us today where we find ourselves constantly overstimulated with a million connections constantly happening at every moment and when we have a portal to all of the information of the world in our pockets.

As we have already seen, people are finding it harder and harder to focus, to be aware, to be present. So how do we get away from this state of constant distraction and semi-attention that so often tips us back into the storms of inner chaos?

Well, obviously we must practise strengthening our attention. This is the key practice of the desert monastic tradition, beginning with the practice of the novice who, in order to rise to the heights of meditative awareness, must begin by being trained in what the early teachers called *proseuchai* (awareness or mindfulness of the present moment as it is) and *nepsis* (inner watchfulness of the thoughts that constantly arise in response to stimuli – this is the famous monkey mind that leads us away from reality and into distraction). When practised over time as the manifestation of our primary intentionality, this focused attention leads to moral discernment, enabling the growth of compassion and *metanoia* – a change of heart that leads to the cultivation of wisdom.

Working on building these two practices as two sides of the 'coin of attention' will enable us to begin letting go of those patterns that do not serve us anymore – letting go of the storms of habitual anxiety, and letting go of those habits of selfishness, self-centredness and egocentric desire that take us from reality as it is in the present moment.

When we let them all go, we move from the false desire that everything would be as we want it, to the true desiring of God as the fulfilment of all desire through the living out of God's will in the moment at hand.

As St Augustine said in *The Confessions*, 'You have made us for yourself, O Lord, and our hearts are restless until they find rest in you.'

Attention as a Practice of Emptiness

This practice of attentiveness, then, becomes our way to emptiness. To focus our attention is to come to the beginning of the path of spiritual *kenosis*, our self-emptying, that purifies our minds and hearts from all that is false. Attending to the moment as it is empties us of desire for it to be anything else, while attending to our thoughts without getting caught up in them allows us to realise that we are not fundamentally our thoughts, or feelings, or sensations. So we empty of a certain false idea of ourself that has been present from the first moment our thinking mind started to chatter back to us. This original emptiness comes about when we rest in the present moment, not seeking anything or wanting anything or even imagining anything but resting in the moment as it arises from Divine Love in its pure origin.

In *The Cloud of Unknowing*, the journey in this direction of attention is taught as the second step towards the meditative state of union, after the cultivation of intention.

At this point in the *Cloud*, via the focusing of attention, we enter what is called the 'cloud of forgetting'. Now, forgetting and attention sound like opposites, but the author means forgetting the distractions in order to be present to reality as it is, and so to the one thing necessary (the transcendent divine origin of reality). Let us look at this practice of forgetting so as to attend, as the author of *The Cloud of Unknowing* defines it.

The Practice of Forgetting

Very beautifully, the author of *The Cloud of Unknowing* says that all thoughts and images of even God and His attributes must be forgotten because, as rational thoughts, no matter how beautiful they may be, they are distractions in themselves in the moment of meditation.

We are not here to think about the Divine but to be present to the Divine relationally in the moment of meditation. To do anything else would be like a lover who sits thinking about the beloved but not attending to the beloved who is with them all along.

So we start by cultivating the 'naked intent' directed to the Divine alone and, finally, we use the practice of a prayer word, a *versiculum* or mantra, to hold us in this awareness of Divine Presence. The *versiculum* is very necessary for the beginner as it gives our rational mind something to work with to lessen the possibility of more distracting thoughts.

Anchoring Our Attention: Using the *Versiculum*

The practice of this (*versiculum*) has been in use within the Christian tradition since the very earliest stages of monastic tradition and roughly corresponds to mantra practices in other traditions. It continues to be taught to this day as part of the discipline of Christian meditation taught by modern schools of practice.

Within the space of attentive meditation, the monastic tradition teaches that we will find that when we rest in focused attention, using the *versiculum* and the breath as anchors holding us in the present moment, then a spaciousness occurs that allows the parallel processes of *kenosis* (the emptying of the false ego self) and *plerosis* (the filling up of the heart with the awareness of Divine Presence) to take place and we are changed. We grow more and more into the divine icon of the Christ we were always meant to be, our being a locus of Divine Presence and Love.

Our contemporary practice of this ancient and powerful discipline invites us to try every day, in every moment, to begin again and again, and to be intent towards the presence of God, aware of what's going on within us and attending to the presence of God, who is with us always. But, of course, if it were that simple, we would all be happy to do it! What about the storm of distractions within? How do we deal with them?

Dealing with Distractions: The Attention Gym

We all have distractions. Today, we are all living in a state of almost maddening distraction most of the time. For the most part, our society today militates against gentle, focused attention. As our meditation practice is a way of attempting to deal with our distracted self, and speaks to the very centre of who we are, then, naturally, the place where we will experience the effects of distraction most fully is when we attempt to sit in attentive meditation.

This experience of distraction can be so bad during meditation that some people will even give up, simply because it brings them a deeper awareness of the distractions around them. Instead, we must realise that the distractions are actually part of the meditative process. This is a very important truth – distraction is necessary to the honing and healing of the faculty of attention.

Distraction is necessary.

There is nothing wrong with distractions as long as you don't cling to them. The constant arrival of distractions and our constant active choice to ignore them during our meditation is the very place where the muscle of meditation is built.

Suppose I was to send you all off to the gym and tell you that you need to build up the muscles in your arms. How would you do that? You would pick up a weight and you would put it down, and then you would repeat this action. You'd pick it up, and you'd put it down. You engage and relax the muscle to strengthen it – and only with both engagement and relaxation over time will the muscle grow.

If you were to walk into the gym and pick up the weight and never put it down again, your arm would simply atrophy, then you would lose all ability to work with it at all.

Distraction works in the same way with the 'mental muscle' of focused attention. We notice a distraction, we return to meditation, we notice a distraction, we return to meditation, we notice the distraction, we return to meditation.

Over years – and it can take years – the power of the distracting thoughts to overcome attention becomes less, the faculty of attention increases and the muscle of our meditative awareness strengthens.

I cannot stress this enough. It is paramount for you, as a person of meditation, to recognise that you cannot grow beyond the broken-minded distracted self that we all experience these days, from the state of semi-attention that we seem to dwell in most of the time, without the distractions.

It should also be remembered that, according to the monastic tradition and its disciplines of dealing with the distractions, the teaching is that as long as you don't grasp at them or cling to them, then they are simply passing thoughts, and thoughts by themselves have no moral value. They are not good or evil in themselves: they are just thoughts. We cannot stop them from arising and it is madness to try.

Instead, we live from the recognition that it is what you do with the thoughts that causes problems. As one of our old friars who taught us in meditation used to say, 'Your mind is like a train station and your thoughts are like the trains coming and going at great speed. In meditation, you are just sitting on the plat-form (resting in the present moment), just watching the trains come and go. As long as you just let them arrive and depart, there's no problem. Just, for good-ness sake, don't get on a train!'

We remember, then, when we go to practice, that distracting thoughts are not evil or virtuous in them-selves. It's what we do with them that counts.

So, we try and work with this process of attention – distraction – return. This practice is the essence of the teaching of the great saintly masters of meditation like St Teresa of Ávila or St Francis de Sales, or so many others who taught that the way we practice is to first consecrate our time to meditation with an act of intention. Then, we sit with God and we say inwardly something like, 'Here I am. I am giving myself completely to you in this time.'

Then, our attention is given over to calm abiding in the presence of God.

Distractions arise but as often as we note them, we come back without judgement, without emotional excitement, without stress or anxiety. We just notice, we let it go, we return.

This constant returning every time we are distracted is all that is asked of us in meditation. The rest of the process belongs to Divine action and grace. As St Francis de Sales in *Introduction to the Devout Life*, writing in the 1500s to beginners on this path of meditation, said: 'If the heart wanders or is distracted, bring it back to the point quite gently and replace it tenderly in its master's presence. And even if you did nothing during the whole of your hour [of meditation] but bring your heart back and place it again in Our Lord's presence, though it went away every time you brought it back, your hour would be very well employed.'

The problem for many meditators is that often they have either never been taught this or they do not believe it, as it can seem, well, just too simple, until you try it and then it is too hard to go on with!

The problem here then is that we are measuring the success of meditation by our own limited understanding, and this can put an unsurmountable burden on us, and particularly on a beginner. *Oh, what's the point in it?* we think. *I go in, I get distracted immediately, I keep losing my thoughts, how can this be a good thing?* It's all okay. You are in the presence of God. As St Teresa d'Ávila reminds us, prayer is a conversation with someone whom I know loves me. As long as you return, and you return gently and without anxiety, all will be well.

Before we finish discussing distractions, there is one other strategy for dealing with them that can be useful and this too is a strategy used by the saints, including extraordinary people of prayer and meditation like St Thérèse of Lisieux. She spoke about her process in *The Story of a Soul* when she was distracted during prayer. 'I also have many [distractions] but as soon as I am aware of them, I pray for those people the thought of whom diverted my attention and, in this way, they reap benefit from my distractions.' This way the distraction is turned in the right way and instead of taking us away from God, it brings us closer to Him.

Whatever distraction we encounter, the remedy is always simply to return to the 'anchors' of our meditation, especially to the prayer word, our *versiculum* or mantra, and to our breath.

We do this to stabilise ourselves in the present moment with awareness and attention so that we may be able to return to our primary intention in the practice to say and live our meditative mission statement, 'Here I am Lord . . . Here I am'.

The most important and indeed consoling thing to remember, of course, is that we all struggle with these experiences. I struggle with it too! Please don't think for a second that because I'm writing this book, I'm some kind of expert at it!

As I've said earlier, it's very easy to teach mindful, meditative prayer, but it's incredibly hard to simply be faithful, to turn up and meditate, to turn up and be present each day. But this fidelity to practice is not just a fidelity to some self-improvement regime: it is a fidelity to love, to God Himself who, whether I am faithful or not to the practice, is always faithful to me, always truly present to me.

Poetry Pause

What If?

Transfiguration
simply meant
seeing things
as they are;
as they really are. . .
Paying prayerful attention
to all things
so
closely,
in the
holy quiet
beyond
distraction's darkening,
that
their being,
bright and shining
and
held in existence
by
Love's
luminous attention,
is revealed.
For,
having climbed
the mountain of prayer,

only
the Apostles
changed,
when with
full awareness,
seeing
Him
as He
really is,
the One who is
the IS
of
all things,
and the Light
by which
we see
light,
they entered
the
divine cloud
and were
themselves
transformed
in their
seeing.

Let's take a moment or two to go through some practices that can help to deal with distractions.

Practice 1: The Practice of Here and Now

Find a comfortable seat in a quiet space, place your feet flat on the floor and your back comfortably straight, take a moment to settle yourself and simply pause.

Rest your hands in your lap and take a moment to become aware of your breath.

Do not change it in any way, but simply notice its rhythm.

Try and become aware of the coolness of the air as it enters your body and the warmth of the air as it leaves your body.

For three cycles of in-breath and out-breath just be with this sensation.

Inwardly, make an act of intention to be present to the moment, or to Divine Presence, in whatever form of words you are comfortable with.

Begin by noticing your bodily sensations.

You may like to begin at the soles of your feet and slowly draw your attention up through your body noticing how sensations enter your awareness. Simply notice them but move on each time.

Watch out for any creation of narrative that happens in your imagination around the sensations.

If narrative begins return to the awareness of the rhythm of your breath and then take up the scanning process again from where you were before the distraction.

Having reached the crown of the head, allow your awareness to rest on your feelings and emotions.

How are you feeling in this moment?

What are your emotions doing in the moment?

Then gently ask the same of your thoughts.

Rest in the observation of your thoughts.

It may help to think of yourself as standing back and watching your thoughts from a distance. See them rise, become present and succeed one another.

Again, if you notice yourself getting drawn into a narrative about the thoughts or about your emotional reaction to the thoughts just return to your breath and the awareness of its rhythm of in and out.

Finally allow your focus to move solely to your breath and to the sounding of your *versiculum* within you. For nine cycles of in-breath and out-breath simply repeat, 'I am here, it is now and I choose to be here in the now.'

As distractions arise, as they will, simply notice them and returned to awareness of the breath and the *versiculum* – 'I am here, it is now and I choose to be here in the now' – without agitation or discouragement.

Practice 2: Walking with Attention

We don't often value the spacious gift that a journey may be. Usually, we are concentrating on the destination as soon as we leave for it, or we may carry an overhang of emotion from the place we have just left. However, a walk that is valued just as a walk is a gift that we can give ourselves, even if we have a destination in mind.

We don't have to walk at a glacial pace either, though it can be nice to slow down and simply wander when we can, enabling that childlike sense of wonder to manifest as we simply absorb what our senses are picking up.

At its most basic, this is simply an exercise of noticing – of honing our attention to notice what is going on around us and within us as we walk, while not becoming attached to any specific sensation.

To begin walking with attention, begin with a moment of stillness in which you make an inner statement of intention. Something simple like, 'Today I choose to walk with attentive awareness and to be open to all that arises along the way.'

As you walk, you may like to start by noticing how you walk.

What leg do you habitually lead off with?

How does the rhythm of your walking feel?

Can you feel the movement of your feet as they roll across the ground or the movement of your body in your clothes as you move?

How does the air feel over your skin?

What is the temperature like?

How is your breathing?

You can then begin to move out of the body's awareness of itself into a wider field of awareness.

What is the surface like to walk on?

Can you feel the difference between road and path?

Is the ground dry or wet?

What is the sky doing?

What sounds can you hear?

What can you smell?

Is there anything or anyone you haven't seen before?

Are there any textures you can reach out and feel safely?

This gentle enquiry as we walk moves us from rumination and narrative thinking into more of a present-moment awareness that hones our attention and enables us to grow into a more open-minded and open-hearted way of being.

We can also add small prayers, verses that help us attend, mantras or compassion practices to our walking by uniting our steps with a prayer to offer our journey for a particular spiritual intention or by choosing to smile at, and inwardly ask blessing for, those we encounter along the way. It is amazing how transformative such a simple practice can become as we learn to open in the moment to the grace of encounter with beauty, compassion and a sense of intention.

Practice 3: Fading into the Background

This is an exercise that can be done in any place. At the beginning I would suggest you try it in a quiet familiar place and then when you are used to it bring it to other places that may be a little more challenging. Personally, I like to do this one when I'm alone in the woods or taking a break on a journey, or even in a busy café, but, with practice, it can be done anywhere, at any time.

In this exercise, we are simply turning up our sensory experience of the environment around us but in a non-narrative, non-judgemental way.

This, in turn, enables us to step out of the false 'me centredness' that we can find ourselves in most of the time. This only sees the world around us as either positive or negative *for* us, individually, rather than as a blessing to be accepted or a challenge to cultivate discernment around.

Find a comfortable seat in a quiet space, place your feet flat on the floor and your back comfortably straight, take a moment to settle yourself and simply pause.

Take a moment to notice how you are feeling, at first in your body, then in your emotions, and, finally, in your mind.

What thoughts are with you at this time? Again, you are just noticing these, not engaging with the sensations or the thoughts.

Notice your breath. Do not change it in any way, just notice.

After a few moments of simply observing your

breath, begin to draw your awareness to the environment around you.

Slowly, visually scan your environment. Stop at anything that engages your attention, but don't name or narrate the engagement. Simply allow it to happen.

When your attention cools towards the focus move on.

As you repeat the slow scan, begin to allow your other senses to do the same.

What is it like to scan the area in an aural or olfactory or tactile way?

Try not to narrate the experience.

If narration or memories or associations arise, return to your breath and begin the scan again.

Notice any details you haven't seen before; notice how your mind tries to pull you towards narration and rumination.

Notice how your field of awareness can expand or retract depending on your level of acceptance of reality as it is or through a veil of rumination.

When your ten minutes is up, slowly reel in your faculty of attention by becoming aware of your breath, then your feet upon the ground and your back against the chair. Finally, take a moment to look around you once again and notice how your perception may have changed.

You can end the practice with a moment of gratitude.

Poetry Pause

Rest

To rest
in the breath
is
to rest
in the
present moment.
To rest
in the present moment
is
to rest
in the now.
To rest
in the now
is
to rest
in the place of possibility.
To rest
in the place of possibility
is
to rest
in the Divine Presence.
To rest
in the Divine Presence
is
to rest

in the Love that *is*.
So then . . .
in every moment
choose
to rest
in your
breath . . .
and your
breath
will become
blessing.

The Precious Present Moment

At the very foundation of our practice of inner attention is an attuning of the self to the present moment.
While all forms of meditation stress the importance
of the present moment as a locus of possibility and
the place of choice, the monastic tradition goes even
deeper in Christianity in its understanding of the
present moment as being a 'sacramental space'. Here
the present moment, when given meditative attention,
opens up and is seen as a place of encounter with the
Divine Now, which in turn radiates out from our
practice to allow us to encounter all that exists as
having an inherent sacramental character too. In other
words, to the practitioner of attentive meditation, in
the everything that exists is a visible sign of an invisible presence.

The practice then is to form our intention clearly and then to dwell in the moment deeply enough, attentively enough (attuned to it through regular meditation practice), so that we are living with the grace of the moment and in the presence of the Divine. When this happens, we find ourselves dwelling more and more in that state of stable equanimity that sees the storms of life calm and a clear sky dawn interiorly once again. As the great twentieth-century poet and meditation teacher Robert Lax said in *The Way of the Dreamcatcher*, 'We must work through our meditation to keep in mind only three things: there is God, you and the moment.'

Now, it takes a lifetime to train yourself to this level of perception of reality, but with discipline and daily repetition of attentive meditation, it can happen. That's why, of course, we speak of ourselves as *practising* meditation, not *succeeding* at it.

In and through the practice of inner attention, we arrive at a way of seeing reality such that the Divine is our only 'where' and the originator of our only 'when'. This will happen if we offer our attentiveness through the intentional practice of recalling ourselves to the conscious awareness of Divine Presence again and again and again.

The quintessential master of this teaching of the sacramentality of the present moment was a Carmelite brother known as Brother Lawrence of the Resurrection, who lived in Paris in the seventeenth century. Some of you reading this may have read his book *The Practice of the Presence of God* – if you haven't, I would heartily recommend it.

The book itself came about because a lady who came to the monastery for spiritual direction from the priests of the community slowly realised that she got more out of her conversations with Brother Lawrence in the kitchen than she did from talking to any of the priests. So, she began to note down the things that Brother Lawrence said and, eventually, she showed it to the superiors in the monastery who realised the gift they had in him and they had these thoughts (along with some letters on prayer he had written and a brief autobiography) published for sharing between the monasteries.

He would no doubt be horrified to know that he has become such an esteemed guide to the spiritual life. Brother Lawrence lived life simply as a cook in the monastery, a place that was in chaos, full of noise and busyness all the time. He spoke of the challenge of retaining an awareness of Divine Presence and his practice of living this awareness on a moment-by-moment basis, of living in the eye of the storm as it were, and so, living in the midst of the busyness and the noise, he could be at peace. This he seems to have done very successfully, so what was his method for keeping this meditative awareness at all times?

The lady describing his activity says that Brother

Lawrence shared that the slightest thing, like flipping the omelette over in the pan, he did deliberately and with intention 'for the love of God'. All of this external but *intentional* business was accompanied by what he called this 'little inward glance' towards God, a moment of pointed, deliberate interior *attention* to the Divine Presence.

He described this little inward glance of the faculty of attention as a 'glance of the heart', which is 'the first of the body's organs to have life and which dominates them all'. This glancing at God is such that it 'imperceptibly kindles a Divine Fire in the soul which blazes up in response'.

We come to realise with Brother Lawrence that no matter the storms that rage around us or within us, there is nothing that can stop us from being tuned into the inner stillness of the calm of Divine Presence if we practice inner attention.

A few years ago, some young people were undertaking one of our meditation courses. One of them was struggling to give up smoking and a teacher suggested to her that she should smoke her next cigarette mindfully, with full meditative attention. She looked at us as though we were crazy, but, the following week, she came back and said that she had been very surprised to discover that when she brought full attention in that moment to the act of smoking, she became very aware that her body 'hated that she smoked'. Her takeaway from the practice was that should she ever really want to give up smoking then she knew that this would work.

When we attend, we become present, and we begin to dwell in the truth of how things actually are.

Blessed Solanus Casey, one of our great brothers well on the way to canonisation, spent forty years as doorkeeper at the St Bonaventure Friary in Detroit. He was a wonderful gentle man, and many miracles of healing were worked through him. On one occasion, one of the friars asked him, 'Solanus, what is your philosophy of life?'

His response was beautiful. 'All that God asks of humanity is that we would be faithful to the present moment.'

Practising Meditative Attention

What, then, are the practices of attention that we may build into our lives in order to dwell in the present moment in such a way that we encounter the presence of God and, by daily practice, remain in that presence?

Earlier we talked about some of the practices of intention, consecration and attention – so what are the practices that you can do in your day-to-day life to keep you attentive and living in the present moment?

Well, you have the basic mindful awareness practices

that we spoke about in our chapter on mindfulness – there we saw the importance of checking in and of seeing how you are in the moment.

To practice meditative attention fully, we combine the practices of mindfulness and inner watchfulness. Watchfulness is cultivating an inner awareness of those thoughts as they pass before the mind's eye, without grasping them or interacting with them, all the while taking refuge in the sanctuary of the breath, enabling the inner life to stabilise. We can also use the *versiculum or mantra* to help us anchor in our present-moment awareness while we watch the thoughts go by.

For example, we can look at the meditative exercise of being with the body in the moment – to be kind to your body in the now. We know that kindness to our body does not mean overindulging it. So, we realise when we are truly attentive, the kindest way of being with our body is to enable it to be healthy and fit and well. So, this leads us to ask the question: 'What do I need to do to be kinder to my body?'

It might be to sleep more, it might be to eat in a different, healthier way, but like that girl who was smoking the cigarette, the important thing is to rest with what actually is and, from there, we begin to discern what God in the present moment is inviting us to do or not do.

The Cultivation of Attentive Stillness: The Telephone Pole Day

When we cultivate this form of attention, we cultivate an awareness of being present deliberately. We may start to take a few minutes of stillness of body and mind that allow us to come to a deeper attentiveness to the present moment. These are touchstone moments when we connect with the self, the moment and the Divine. But we must begin gently. At the beginning, even three minutes is enough. Don't start by thinking you are going to sit in stillness for half an hour – if you're not used to it, you'll be bouncing off the walls within ten minutes! No. We grow our practice gently. We establish a practice of taking moments of stillness and quiet throughout the day.

One of my great teachers in meditation described this as the 'telephone pole theory'. Let me explain.

Imagine your day as a long road along on which you are travelling.

Alongside the road, there are telephone poles at regular intervals, connected by wires.

The telephone poles are the intentional moments of meditative awareness we put in throughout the day; the wires carry the 'signal' of connection to God from moment to moment and the 'signal' is maintained throughout the day. There are two dangers to be avoided, however – and both of them are mistakes often made by beginners in the way of attentive meditation.

The first is to have too many 'poles'. The wire

becomes taut, stretched too tightly, and eventually breaks and contact is lost. This is the mistake made by those who are overenthusiastic and want to do too much too soon. They become exhausted quickly.

The other extreme is when we put in too few 'poles'. This is the mistake made by those who like the idea of practising meditation, but only do so when they feel the need to. The wires are stretched, sag and eventually break and contact is lost once more.

So, the advice, then, is to begin with a regular but simple number of practices that do not tire you too much, and enable you to gently but consciously return to the present moment each time. And so the advice is to begin by bringing our faculty of attention to things we are already doing regularly but to now invest them with spiritual attention. This could be our mindful, meditative walk or preparing our food or listening to a friend.

Of course, each person must find their own balance, which will be unique to each of us, but we can at least look at what the tradition teaches about the best and most essential practices. These include the consecration practices (mentioned on p 149) and the forming of solid habits of practice through regular times of attentive meditation. However, if we really want to see these moments of meditation become transformative, we must deepen the practice of inner watchfulness to look at the roots of our behaviour.

Deepening Inner Watchfulness: Examining the Roots

One of the more important practices that arises from our practice of attentiveness is interior watchfulness. This is a meditative examination that goes beyond a basic examination of conscience. It's not about what I did or didn't do, instead, it's about recognising the problems we are struggling with but also recognising the graces and the good in our lives and valuing them, naming them.

Even more than that, it asks what is at the root of the moral choices we make. Often, the moral event and the roots of the choices we make can be at some remove from one another, and only real meditative awareness shone inwardly will enable us to discover the 'why' of the event at hand.

Real interior watchfulness will enable us to catch the moment that the action (or reaction) becomes possible and even inevitable, thus enabling us to decide mindfully and to choose clearly and according to the illumination of the conscience by the light of meditative awareness.

For example, some of the biggest reactions to stimuli or habitual patterns begin with much simpler experiences such as boredom or hunger or tiredness. Boredom begets agitation, the agitation becomes fantasy, fantasy triggers patterns, and when we've entered a pattern it is almost inevitable for the action to take place and it moves into reality very quickly.

To practise our awareness, to watch the thoughts as they arise while dwelling in attentive meditation enables, over time, a deep change and transformation to take place. We soon find that the more we choose to dwell in the awareness of the present moment, the more room for choice we have.

The Practice of the *Versiculum*

As described on p. 89, the practice of the *versiculum* (little word) is one of the key anchors of prayer that keeps us attentive to the present moment.

When the Desert Fathers and Mothers taught this form, they would speak of verses of scripture that were appropriate in different ways at different times. The most common one that they used was taken from the Psalms, and it's one we still use in the Divine Office (the regular daily prayer times celebrated by monastics) and the Rosary: 'Oh God, come to our assistance. O Lord, make haste to help us' (Psalm 69:2).

One of the early fathers says to use that verse, but if that's not working say, 'Lord, enlighten my darkness!' and, in terrible moments when nothing seems to work, just simply cry out 'Jesus, Jesus!'

It was from that crying out to Jesus and the understanding of the power of the Holy Name, that the practice of the Jesus Prayer, the use of the Holy Name itself as the *versiculum*, began.

All of these meditative practices work hard to establish the mind in stability and stillness and attentiveness to the present moment. The practice, then, is a simple one in its essence.

Practice: Combining Intention and Attention

We have formed our intention and wish to live the meditation way.

Find a comfortable seat in a quiet space, place your feet flat on the floor and your back comfortably straight, take a moment to settle yourself and simply pause.

Start by stating this intention. 'Lord, I dedicate this time in this space and my own personhood to you . . . Here I am.'

Become aware of your breath.

Follow its ebb and flow.

Feel its movement in your body.

While being attentive to your breath as a gift from Divine Love, slowly add to it the *versiculum* that feels right to you.

Allow your breath and the word to be your anchors in the present.

Let them become your point of connective awareness to the Divine.

Repeat the word and remain with your breath.

Let the breath and the word fall into a natural rhythm of breathing the word.

If distractions come, notice them, let them go and return to the present with attention renewed each time as you return to the word and the breath.

Watch thoughts, feelings and sensations arise without becoming attached to them or entering into conversation with them.

Again and again return yourself to the word and the breath.

When you are comfortable to do so, you can allow the word to fade into silence and just be with the breath.

Begin to listen to the sounds around you once more, and feel your feet on the floor and your back against the chair.

Finish with a prayer or thought of gratitude

Dealing with Distractions: The Gift of Boredom

The early monks sometimes spoke of what they called the 'noonday devil', which often affected those who were dedicated to meditation. The technical term for it is *acedia*. It is defined as the boredom that strikes within a repetitive practice and tempts the practitioner to give up their practice and do something 'more useful'.

The image often used to illustrate this was the monk in the desert who spent most of his meditation willing 'the sun to move' (willing time to pass more quickly), so his practice would be over and he could return to the 'real life' of work.

At some point, you will find this in your own meditation, where you think, 'That's it, I must have done my fifteen minutes by now!' You look at the clock and only five minutes have gone by!

Acedia is described as the distraction that was the most difficult but also the most important to overcome in meditative practice, as it manifests as a boredom that demands movement under the cover of virtue.

'My practice feels very dry today so, instead of sitting, I think I'll go and I'll read something that might spur me back on track.'

'I will go down to the kitchen and I'll get a cup of coffee and I'll drink that and then I'll come back to practice because I'll be much more awake' . . . and so on.

The essential element is the idea that we are moved to promise ourselves that we can always practise better if we practise later.

To warn against this idea, there was a lovely story of a monk who kept saying that he could always pray later. He died suddenly one day, having never returned to meditation, and his guardian angel whispered into his ear, 'No more later!'

At that moment, you're into the eternal now and you don't have the chance to start practising again. So, we practise now and, in the now, recognise that we only have this moment to practise. No other moment is guaranteed.

Acedia, then, is characterised by the monastic who looks out his window all day to see if anybody is in need of help, rather than meditating and trusting that if someone does need help, they will be shown a path to his door.

Now, the monastic teachers say the only thing that should draw us from our prayer is a brother or a sister who is in need – in which case, if a brother or a sister is in need, it is Jesus in them seeking our help and our assistance – but we don't go looking for the brother or sister in need during meditation time! If we do, then we are really seeking distraction as opposed to an opportunity to practise real compassion.

The only real remedy for acedia is to cultivate the discipline of meditation, for us to abide in practice regularly and, no matter what, for us to continue unless genuine charity calls us away.

Dealing with Distractions: Sleep

This is the one distraction many beginners get torn up about. Until you begin a meditative practice in earnest, your body thinks any sustained period of relaxation is a pathway to sleep, and so at the start you can find it difficult to stay awake. This is where adopting the alert and aware meditation postures we spoke of on page 91 really help.

However, if you fall asleep, that's OK, as long as

you return to practice as soon as you can and don't disturb others.

When we go back to our Desert Fathers, there's one story of a monk who comes to his elder and he says, 'Abba, that monk who is with me in the cell begins to fall asleep every time we sit down to meditate, and slowly he slides down the wall until his head is resting on my shoulder and it disturbs my prayer. May I have permission to correct him?'

The Abba says, 'No, you may not. But the next time you go to the chapel you are to tie a pillow to your shoulder!' Compassion for the tired practitioner is always important

Other Forms of Attentive Meditation

There are many other forms of meditation within the tradition that will help us to improve our ability to live intentionally and with inner attention. These include methods like focusing on a sacred object and, through this, coming to rest in our being with the Divine Presence at its centre.

We begin by recognising that the gaze of Divine Love is holding that object in existence. In these forms, we may use candles or icons or even just the contemplation of the beauty of creation itself. The Divine Mystery can be approached through contemplating the tree, the animal or the landscape with focused attention and then, like St Francis, finding in them the *vestigia dei*, the marks or the fingerprints of the Creator.

The Rosary

Another form of prayer that we that we may follow as a deep practice of Christian meditation is the Rosary.

In Ireland, they used to say that you may pray the Rosary to remember or you may pray the Rosary to forget. To pray to remember was to meditate upon the 'mysteries' of the Rosary, the important events in the life of Christ and His Blessed Mother. This was imaginal, discursive, meditative prayer, often done as a form or Lectio. To pray to forget meant to forget the self and the distractions of the mind and heart, allowing the beads and the repetition of the prayers, the 'Our Father', the 'Hail Mary', the 'Glory Be', to become mantras of the prayer of calm abiding, contemplatively resting your 'Here I am' in the perfect 'Yes' of Mary to the Divine Will.

Combining, as it does, both sides of the meditative tradition, the Rosary is seen as one of the deepest schools of contemplative practice in our tradition because it leads us from imaginal discursive prayer into meditative silence and stillness, into the embrace of the Mother who leads us to the Christ who calms the storms of our broken being with total love.

We had a lovely old brother for many years named Seraphin. He was an extraordinary contemplative, one of the greatest masters of meditation I have ever met. Though he would roll over in his grave if he thought I was describing him as such. But he prayed the Rosary constantly. He wore his beads on his habit cord and you would see no matter what he was doing he was telling the beads through his fingers while working. One day, I noticed that it was quite a battered old rosary. There were beads missing and there were links gone and, as I used to make rosaries, I said to him, 'Brother, would you like me to repair your rosary?'

'You will not!' He smiled. 'It would take me twice as long if all the beads were back!'

Poetry Pause

Beads

I want
my whole day
to be
a rosary
of presence.
Each bead
a moment
of awareness
strung together

on
the chain of breath,
passing between
the fingers
of attention,
bringing down
Heaven
in my
Joys,
Sorrows,
Lights,
Glories,
connecting
earth and life,
mothering
the new
and the possible
into being,
born again
and again
until
death
bears me
into
Life,
until the chain
of time
breaks,
and the beads

of experience
are worn away
to
silence.
But
for now,
distracted
and
discordant
as I am,
I pick up
the beads
once more
and begin
again.

Visio Divina

Then, we have the various forms of imaginative or visualising forms of meditation. In these forms, we imagine ourselves in a particular scene, perhaps a scene from the gospel, that we enter into while speaking with Jesus.

This isn't some kind of false delusion or getting lost in a kind of hallucinatory practice. Rather, it enables the Divine Presence to use the faculty of our imagination to teach us and grant us insight and wisdom arising from the union of our life with these images.

In all of this we are not looking for visionary experiences and we are certainly not dictating what God should be saying to us. Rather, it should be seen more as holding up a picture (my own life) to the light of Divine Love in order to see more clearly the detail of the picture in hand. This leads us to cultivating the sanctification and the purification of the imagination, which St Teresa of Ávila herself said is one of the key tools for meditative prayer.

Here are two practices of basic imaginal meditation.

Practice 1: The Inner Sky

Find a comfortable seat in a quiet space, place your feet flat on the floor and your back comfortably straight, take a moment to settle yourself and simply pause.

Consciously invite Divine Love to guide your meditation.

Move through the basic listening form of relaxation.

Begin by listening to the noises furthest away.

Now the noises in your room or building.

Now the noise of your own breath.

Without changing them, notice the rhythm and sensations of your breathing.

We move into deep body relaxation.

Breathing out all tension and stress (I like to visualise this as fog that dissolves in sunlight).

Breathing in relaxation and peace (I like to visualise this as light that warms).

Imagining I am lying on my back in a green field on a beautiful summer's day.

Imagine the sensations of such an experience.

I watch the clouds come and go.

As they pass over me, I experience their shadow and the coolness that goes with it.

But the sun still shines behind the clouds.

Ask the inner question, 'If your heart is like the sky, what is your inner weather like at the moment?'

Was it different this morning?

Will it be different later?

Make a statement: 'My awareness is like the sun, always there and always peaceful even above my inner weather. My awareness rests in the peace of Christ or Divine Love.'

Gently allow the images to fade and return to the awareness of your breath.

Return to the awareness of your feet on the floor.

End with a moment of thanksgiving.

Practice 2: The Inner Sanctuary Meditation

Find a comfortable seat in a quiet space, place your feet flat on the floor and your back comfortably straight, take a moment to settle yourself and simply pause.

Invite the presence of Divine Love to guide your meditation.

Move through the basic listening form of relaxation.

Notice the noises furthest away.

Then, the noises in the room.

Then, the noise of your own breath.

Be with the sensations of breathing

We move into deep body relaxation.

Breathing out tension and stress as smoke that dissolves.

Breathing in relaxation and peace as light that warms.

Now we follow the light of the breath to the centre-point of the rhythm of the breath.

To the place where the in-breath becomes the out-breath and the out-breath becomes the in-breath.

Really notice that place.

As you follow your breath to that centre point, begin to see a door appear in front of you.

This is the door to your inner sanctuary.

To your inner place of peace where Divine Love dwells holding you in being.

In your imagination, because everything is possible in your imagination, walk up to the door.

Gently breathing in and out.

What does the door look like?

What is it made of?

Imagine you reach out and touch it?

The door is locked but you will always have the key to it.

Look down in your hand and watch the key appear.

Unlock the door and push it open.

Step through the door into your inner sanctuary, your inner room.

This is your place to be peaceful.

This is your place to be calm.

This is your place to abide with the Divine Presence who always abides here in peace.

So, however you want it to look, that's how it looks.

Have a look around you.

What does it look like? Sound like? Smell like?

Is it indoors or outdoors?

Is there furniture?

However you want to design it so you can be peaceful there, you can do so.

Ask yourself: 'What needs to be here so I can be peaceful today?'

Say to yourself: 'I am here. It is now. I choose to be here in the now in my inner sanctuary in God's presence.'

Gently breathe in and out.

Only you can come in here.

No other human being can ever enter your inner sanctuary.

Sit down in your inner sanctuary and relax there.

See how your breathing has calmed and slowed now that you are here.

Feel your body relax and become calm.

Gently watch your thoughts as they come and go like the weather.

Gently breathing in and out.

Know that whenever you want to come back here you can do so by just listening to your breathing and following your breath to the door.

The door will always be there waiting for you.

The key will always appear in your hand.

Gently breathe in and out.

Now, get up and take a look around your inner sanctuary again.

Then begin to walk towards the door.

When you get to the door take one last look back at your sanctuary.

Remember it will always be here waiting for you.

Go through the door.

Close it.

Lock it with your key.

Allow the key to disappear.

It will always reappear when you come to the door.

Watch the door fade into the light of your breath.

Gently breathe in and out.

Now begin to listen to the sound of your breath again.

Feel your feet against the floor.

Feel your back against the chair.

Offer your practice of thanksgiving.

Return and shake out and stretch.

present moment and then we are inspired by that love to become more than we ever thought possible. I hope you have met people like this. We feel more peaceful when we're with them. They raise us up. They invite us into a deeper awareness and, if we are very blessed, they are in our lives in such a way that we can have a regular connection with them.

If you know people like this, if you're thinking of people you know who are like this right now, then please go and be with them, as they have so much to teach even though they teach not by talking but just by being around us, by being with us.

We can become that person too by allowing our practice to overflow and transform into compassionate action that reaches out through us to those in need.

Poetry Pause

The Quiet Ones

There are quiet saints everywhere.
Hidden in plain sight, they do their work
gently and slowly and lovingly.
Repairing the world over and over again.
Despite the pain, despite the sadness
at the heart of it all.
Despite not even knowing
that this is their work.

You know them.
We all do.
The barely remembered face
on the bus that gave a word of advice
that carried you for a while.
The beggar who smiled
from the street corner you rushed past,
whether you gave or didn't.
The teacher who took time with you
until the light finally dawned within.
The old lady who promised
she would light a candle
for you, and did.
The tired nurse who,
nonetheless, held your hand.
The old man who showed you
how to plant an acorn.
The child who smiled at you
when you didn't feel worthy
of such a gift.
All of them, punctuation points
of grace in the story of
your gradual unfolding.
Their numbers swell the world,
silently, secretly,
and ensure the sun
comes up for one more day.
That the moon rises
for one more night,

and that hope is possible for
one more hour.
Their kindness is a tide
stronger than the sea,
and just as relentless
in its constant return.
They reflect light into
the night window of your soul
as gently as the Moon
falling on silvered waters.
You may never know
their names.
Yet they have mended
the frayed edges of your life
more often than
you will ever know.
They have seen you,
and in the moment
of their seeing,
you have felt seen,
known, loved,
necessary, meaningful,
even if just for a moment.
They may be beside you right now.
They may be sitting in your café,
or be alongside you
on the bus-stop bench,
or be just behind you
in the queue,

or just in front.
Here is how you will know them:
They smile often with their eyes,
and with their souls.
They have borne great suffering
without becoming hard or cold.
They disappear quickly.
Fading like Angels do,
having delivered their good news.
Their Gospel is kindness.
Their eyes, no matter their age,
are those of dancing children.
Their smile true and hard won.
They are often very old,
or seeming so, or very young.
They speak less about themselves
and listen more than you or I.
They pray and breathe
as if they are one thing.
They laugh and cry
deeply, and often,
without ever becoming
stuck in either.
They come when needed,
though often
at the last minute,
but always on time.
They twinkle as
the first and the last star does.

They wear wisdom
as lightly as summer rain.
They give their gift
unminding of its value.
They let you walk away
in peace.
They walk on as blessing.
There are quiet saints
everywhere.
Perhaps you have met one?
Perhaps you could become
one?

The whole purpose of all of this practising is to hear the call of the holy men and women of all ages and places in our own hearts, to hear the call of Christ in our hearts. When our mind–heart centredness attends to the presence through meditation, we find, as Isaiah says, 'that you keep them in perfect peace whose mind is stayed on you' (Is 26:3). The experience of this peace and equanimity even in the midst of our own storms becomes a practice of compassion in its own right as we share it and live it with others. Indeed, I would go so far as to say that the presence and growth of compassion (or its absence) is a clear indication of whether someone's practice of intentionality and attentive meditation is actually proceeding as it should. One of the key ways we can measure this compassion as a fruit of our practice is to see how readily we leap to the judgement of others. Hopefully our meditation will be so attentive that we will see how broken and fallible we are ourselves, which in turn will generate compassion towards all others in an empathetic way. Prejudices must be uncovered, challenged and released if we are to truly walk the meditative path. Awareness and inner watchfulness are key here as sometimes they can manifest even under the disguise of wanting to do the right thing. True compassion, informed by true meditative practice, arises instead from acceptance of the present moment as it is and a seeking for the revelation of the Divine within it. A little story from the monastic tradition may help to illustrate this.

We Three Adore You Three: A Story of Compassion Awakened

Let us begin with a newly ordained bishop.

Being a new bishop, he was being very careful about his work and he decided he must fulfil all of the pastoral ministry of the bishop, so he planned to tour his diocese.

Some days into his journey, he came to a monastery. He was delighted that he had a monastery in his diocese, because the monks would pray for him and for the success of his mission. So, he went into the monastery and met the abbot and all the monks, and they had a lovely time together. They prayed together and they celebrated mass together. It was all wonderful and a very joyous occasion, and the monks were delighted that their new bishop was with them.

As the visit was concluding and he was about to leave, the abbot asked, 'Are you not going to meet the hermits we have?'

The bishop was astounded! Hermits in his diocese, another blessing!

The abbot told him to look out the window where he would see, just off the coast, a little island where, some thirty years earlier, three monks had decided they wanted to live in deeper meditation without any distractions.

They had been given permission by his predecessor and off they had gone and there they lived. From time to time, supplies were rowed out to them, but they hadn't been seen in a long time. They simply lived there in constant meditation.

The bishop absolutely wanted to meet them. So, he went into the boat and they rowed him out and he found the little hut that the hermits lived in and he met the three most bedraggled-looking individuals he had ever seen in his life.

He was wearing beautiful new purple robes and he looked at these three silent souls, who didn't seem to have even noticed him, and he said to himself, 'Why did I even come out here? They're dirty and they don't seem to be with it really at all.'

Anyway, he talked to the monks and taught them and the three hermits sat there, just listening.

Finally, he told them that he had finished teaching and that they would end with some prayer. Now, they looked interested, and he began to pray the 'Our Father'.

But the three monks looked at him in silence.

The bishop paused and said, 'Do you not know the "Our Father"?'

They shook their heads and one said, 'Oh, well, we used to know it, but we don't remember it anymore.'

'What about the "Hail Mary" or the "Glory Be"?' said the bishop, now aghast. 'Surely you know them at least?'

They shook their heads with a smile.

Well, he was the bishop after all, so he began to teach them. He drilled them in the 'Our Father', in the 'Hail Mary', in the 'Glory Be', until they were word perfect.

Finally, he asked the three hermits, 'But how do you pray every day?'

And together they said, 'We pray like this.'

And the three of them prostrated themselves on the ground and said, 'We three adore you three, have mercy on us for we are sinners.' They told him they had repeated this over and over until it became silence.

'But that's not a prayer,' said the bishop, horrified. 'Stand up!'

He went through the prayers again with them, over and over until they finally remembered. Finally, the bishop went to leave, he gave them his blessing, got into the boat and took off across the bay to return to the monastery where he decided he was going to have to talk to the abbot about these three mad hermits.

But a huge storm blew up! The boat was tossed here and there, they could not get to the coast, and the poor bishop thought, *Is this it, Lord?* He was praying and calling out to God for help. Suddenly, he saw, away across the bay, a little point of light and it seemed to be very calm where the light was . . .

It seemed to be spreading out towards him and, in the middle of the light, he saw the three hermits and they were walking across the water towards the boat. They got to the side of the boat and they smiled at the bishop. Suddenly, all was calm around the boat again.

The bishop said, 'You've come to save me!'

But the three hermits looked surprised and said, 'No, we just can't remember those prayers that you taught us . . . can you go through them again?'

The bishop said, with tears in his eyes, 'When you pray, simply say, "We three adore you three, have mercy on us for we are sinners." That is all.'

This is what we mean by true meditative awareness of Divine Presence that leads to real compassion. This is what anchoring ourselves in Divine Love does and this is what allowing ourselves to be in utter simplicity before the Lord achieves. This is what it really is all about – at the essence of things, at the centre of things – a communion with the God who is, moment by moment, and then finding within ourselves a rising tide of compassion that overflows out into the service of all, but especially of those most in need, not in a patronising or paternalistic way but as a privileged place of encounter with the Divine.

The time has come to go a little deeper into our contemplative tradition, and also to look at some of the aids that the tradition provides for us in terms of anchoring ourselves firmly and fully in the present moment as that place of Divine Encounter, that place where the storms are calmed and the light of Divine Love dawns.

Meditative Relationality as a Practice of Compassion

We have, then, established ourselves in mindful awareness that leads to the practice of compassionate service. We are living with the awareness of the Divine Presence in ourselves, and this leads us into an awareness of recognising that there are positives and negatives in our lives as we lead them.

We then begin to look beyond the surface of those positives and negatives, to look at the conditions that lead to them. As I've said in Chapter 1, mindfulness is only the first step in our meditative life. Eventually, we also look at inner watchfulness too – the meditation practice that sits with the reality of our lives as they are at the moment, including its moral and relational dimensions – and we ask: How can it be better?

This, in turn, leads to deeper questions.

- How can I begin to abandon negative patterns of behaviour that are harming me and/or others? How can I see transformation take place?

- How can I ensure that, in the midst of knowing my brokenness more fully, I can see that compassion is generated for all other beings as well?

Meditation invites us into growth and a deep awareness of our interbeing, the fact that our existence is dependent on the great web of life all around us. We move into that life of service, that life of 'shalom', of integrated peace, where we are in a right relationship with God, with ourselves, with others and with the cosmos at large; thus an ecological compassion is born in us also.

The following practices are short and simple ways for us to connect to this ever-more-needed experience of stillness that brings real calmness to the storms of life and allows space in which compassion for ourselves and for all beings may arise.

Here are nine short ways to drop into stillness.

Practice 1: The Purposeful Pause

Stop what you are doing.

If possible stand up or find a comfortable seat in a quiet space, place your feet flat on the floor and your back comfortably straight, take a moment to settle yourself and simply pause.

Take a moment to become aware of your breath.

Follow its cycle of in-breath and out-breath, watching out for the moment when one yields to the other.

Gently bring your hands up to chest height and then slowly bring your palms together into a prayer pose.

Hold this position for three cycles of in-breath and out-breath.

Gently release your palms and slowly drop your arms.

Take a deep breath in and a deep breath out.

Smile.

Return to your activity.

Practice 2: Checking In

Stop what you are doing.

Find a comfortable seat in a quiet space, place your feet flat on the floor and your back comfortably straight, take a moment to settle yourself and simply pause.

Sitting quietly and gently, turn your awareness to your breath.

When you are fully aware of the ebb and flow of your breathing, ask yourself the question: 'How am I in this moment?'

Allow a few moments of stillness after you ask the question and see what arises in your mind.

Do not judge or censor your impressions.

Gently ask yourself: 'How am I in my body in this moment?'

Allow time to notice your body's reply through its sensations.

Gently ask yourself: 'How am I in my feelings in this moment?'

Allow your feelings the space and time they need to arise and disappear.

Gently ask yourself: 'How are my thoughts in this moment?'

Notice what your mind is giving energy and time to.

Return to your breath for three cycles of in-breath and out-breath.

Finish by inwardly resolving to listen to your body, your heart and your mind a little more deeply each day.

Smile.

Return to your activity.

Practice 3: Fast Mindful Walking

When there are times that you must walk quickly and purposefully, you can still do this mindfully with this ancient technique.

As you begin to walk, gently watch the change in your breath rhythm as it moves from slow to fast, or from shallow to deep.

As you walk, notice the rhythm of your stride – how your left hand rises with your right leg and vice versa.

As each hand rises, gently press the pad of your thumb to the pad of your middle finger and, as you do so, inwardly say your prayer word.

A similar approach may be used if you jog or run during the times that you are slowing down to a walking pace or speeding up to run.

Practice 4: The Holy Object

During times of stress, when our practice isn't as stable as it normally would be, it can be good to carry a small object with us to act as another anchor of practice. This can be a holy object, such as a rosary or crucifix, or even a simple natural object, like a smooth pebble from the beach.

When we have to face into stressful situations, our object becomes our touchstone, reminding us of the depth of our practice and the Divine Presence we are dwelling in.

Find a comfortable seat in a quiet space, place your feet flat on the floor and your back comfortably straight, take a moment to settle yourself and simply pause.

Place the object in your hand.

Simply holding the object as we enter into the situation will enable us to connect powerfully to our practice and to recall us to the stability of our breath and the calmness of our sitting in Divine Presence.

One note! If you choose a natural object like a pebble, remember there is no power or virtue in the stone itself, but only in it as a focal point of prayerful attention. In fact, you should change the stone often, so as not to get too attached or dependent on the stone itself. It is simply an anchor holding us close to our practice.

Practice 5: Mindful Stretching – Sitting Position

Today, we all move too little. This can cause our breath to become stagnant as well as causing many other small ailments. Remember, the freer and deeper your breath, the more stable and relaxed you will become.

Stop all activity and find a comfortable seat in a quiet space, place your feet flat on the floor and your back comfortably straight, take a moment to settle yourself and simply pause.

Notice your body's posture. Are you cutting off your breath because you are slouching or squashing your belly or diaphragm?

Imagine a hook connecting with the crown of your head and gently pulling you up into a straight but relaxed position, such that your lungs are free to breathe to their full capacity.

Gently and slowly exhale fully.

Pause for a count of three.

Gently and slowly inhale fully.

Repeat this three times.

Return to normal breathing.

Offer a prayer of thanksgiving for the gift of your body.

Smile.

Practice 6: Mindful Stretching – Standing Position

Find a comfortable seat in a quiet space, place your feet flat on the floor and your back comfortably straight, take a moment to settle yourself and simply pause.

Gently stand up.

Take a moment to scan your body.

Notice if you are leaning forwards or backwards, to the right or to the left.

Gently correct this, so that you are standing straight with your feet about hip-width apart.

Unlock your knees so that they are loose but not bent.

As you breath out, fully sink slightly on your knees.

As you breathe in, fully rise slightly and allow your arms to leave your sides and slowly stretch up towards the sky.

Repeat this action three times.

Gently swivel on your hips to the left and to the right.

Repeat this three times.

Pause now to breathe and to scan your body again.

Notice if you feel any different.

Press your palms together and offer a prayer of thanksgiving.

Smile.

Relax.

Practice 7: The Mindful Shower

Even a quick morning shower can be a mindful way of entering your practice.

As you enter the shower, take a deep breath and be thankful for the gift of clean water with which to bathe.

Notice how your body responds to the water.

Notice the smells of the shampoo and shower gel and the associations they have or the effect they have on you.

Be happy that you are able to care for your body in this way.

Listen to the sounds of the water and inhale the steam deeply.

If thoughts, worries or plans are present in your mind, note them and then let them go by returning to the sensations of the shower.

When you leave the shower, notice the difference in the way your body feels.

As you dry your body, feel the texture of the towel or the coolness of the air or the different textures of your clothes.

We enter the present moment through our senses.

When all is finished, take a moment for three cycles of in-breath and out-breath, offer a prayer of thanksgiving and smile deeply.

Practice 8: A Mindful Journey

Choose one journey a week and take it mindfully. It may be a familiar journey you take every day or one that you have never had to make before. What matters is the attention you bring to it.

Before you begin, find a comfortable seat in a quiet space, place your feet flat on the floor and your back comfortably straight, take a moment to settle yourself and simply pause. Take some time to breathe and allow your breath to slow, deepen and drop into your belly.

Then begin.

Remember, the goal of the exercise is to notice as much as you can about your environment without moving into rumination on the past or fantasy or worry about the future.

But if you find you have lost focus along the way, simply pause, breathe deeply, invite the presence of the Holy Spirit and your guardian angel, and begin again.

Remind yourself along the way: 'What can I see/ smell/touch/taste/feel/hear at this point?'

Look above and below your usual eyeline especially. If you meet others along the way, smile at them and notice their reaction in a non-judgemental way.

When you reach your destination, take a moment to smile and be thankful for all that you have noticed.

Practice 9: Mindful Handwashing

This exercise is a mindful way of touching gratitude and healing and is an act of compassion towards ourselves.

When you next have to wash your hands and have a few minutes, begin by taking a deep breath.

As the water runs, notice its temperature and the feeling it gives as it touches your hands.

Be thankful for the gift of running water.

As you wash your hands, remember all the people who have touched your hands with kindness or whom you have touched with kindness over the years.

Remember those who have washed you when you were an infant and think about those who will wash you when you are no longer able to do so for yourself.

Allow a sense of connection and gratitude to arise

in your heart for all those who have shown you care and kindness.

Realise they are instruments of Divine Compassion and Peace.

As you dry your hands, remember that you begin life in the care of others and you end life in the care of others, and, in between, we are called to care for others.

Before leaving the bathroom, take three cycles of breath and resolve to bring the spirit of gratitude and care with you.

You may like to end this practice with the prayer of gratitude for water taken from the Canticle of St Francis: 'Be praised, my Lord, for our Sister Water, so very useful and humble and precious and chaste.'

Dwelling in Meditative Awareness

People often ask how they can remain in this compassionate state of awareness.

Could they do their exercise meditatively and with compassion?

Could they do their gardening meditatively and with compassion?

Could they do their work or raise their family meditatively and with compassion?

The answer is simply, yes, of course you can. Anything that we do can be done meditatively and with compassion.

Simple mindfulness practices and the deeper meditation of the breath and even of the prayer word (*versiculum*) may accompany us into any activity and there bear the fruit of compassionate action. Like Brother Lawrence, you can flip the omelette for the love of God (or cut the grass or exercise or work or raise a family). To live this way leads us into the practice of simple gentle adoration, where we are present to God in the present moment, gazing on Him as He gazes on us and holds us in return, and then empowered by our practice to reach out to others in compassion and service.

WISDOM

When talking about wisdom as the fourth inner direction of our meditation map, we do not mean the mere increase of knowledge, though we will certainly learn many new things along the way, nor do we mean simply becoming proficient in meditative techniques. To live with wisdom, to become wise, in its fullest and most sacred sense, is the real goal of our lives according to many of the meditative traditions. Indeed, we can say that most traditional views of our human lives have, as their goal or end state, a dwelling in some form of transcendent wisdom that enables us to attain the fullness of human living.

Many traditional depictions of the life cycle see the

first stage of our existence as a struggle for survival – we struggle to be born, to grow, to achieve independence and individuation. Midlife is seen as the time of creativity, whether of a family, a career or some meaningful contribution to human society. Finally, the ultimate end goal is to become – by virtue of our meditative work, which should be learned and engaged with throughout these former stages, or at the very least from the time we enter this third stage – a wise person. This is someone we would have called a sage, or in the Christian tradition a saint.

So how do we accomplish this journey towards wisdom?

Firstly, it is important to say that there is no need to run away from your ordinary life. Instead, we recognise a call within the present moment to live with the reflective capacity fully engaged. If we do not live this way, our lives become a series of events characterised by a concentration on the way those events make us feel, rather than a transformational process that slowly works with Divine Love to enable us to live in a flow of gradual discernment, learning and conscious change, to reach our fullest potential.

Without the pursuit of wisdom – without the mindful, meditative reflection that is necessary in its pursuit – your life without these meditative disciplines, without the pursuit of wisdom as a goal, is a life that succumbs easily to the storms that rage around, and even within, our human life. And our life becomes a series of unconnected events rather than a life of meaning leading to wisdom.

To understand this a little more fully, let us return for a moment to those storms of mind, heart, soul and life that we find ourselves beset by so often. Now the instinct of most people when they see a storm on the horizon is to try to run from it. This is disastrous. We will exhaust ourselves and will always be living in fear of the next storm. However, those who pursue the art of meditation realise that storms in life are inevitable and escape is impossible, and so instead they seek the eye of the storm – that place of perfect stillness and perfect awareness that exists at the heart of even the wildest hurricane.

When we reach the eye of the storm, we become like Elijah the prophet whose life as told in the first book of Kings in the Old Testament is a wonderful map of the whole process of the meditative process.

Worn out from the storms of his own life, Elijah is finally called to the mountain of God (the heights of meditative practice), there to wait for the revelation of God. (I Kings 6) We are told that, sitting in stillness, he is beset firstly by a great wind, then a powerful earthquake and, finally, a burning fire. Traditionally, these three forces have been seen as the great storms of life that attack those who meditate. The howling winds are the thoughts that distract us, the earthquake is the shock of the dissolution of the ego and false self that always wants to be at the centre of all things, and, finally, the fire is the burning of desire that our reality be other than it is in the present moment.

Elijah learned to abide, to practise his deep sitting and waiting on Divine Love, and so all of those chaotic energies arise within and around him but, without his attention feeding them, they come and they go. He abides at the still centre, he does not engage with them or feed them or even reject them, he simply waits on God. He has arrived at the beginning of the way of wisdom. So when the gentle murmuring of God's voice is finally heard, he realises that it has been there all along.

In our meditative practice, as we pursue true wisdom, we discover that this in-breathing of Divine Love is the background music of our lives and bestows the gift of transcendent meaning. But, when we become lost in the storms, we lose our ability to hear it and so we tumble from storm to storm, often overwhelmed by our experiences and our traumas or lost in anxiety about the future. Only from the still centre – from the very eye of the storm – will wisdom arise and the storms of our lives blow themselves out. They become calm when we stop feeding them with chaotic thoughts, false notions of ourselves and others, and false desires.

We seek this still centre by our practice of clear intentionality, attentive meditation arising from mindful awareness, and we abide there by the daily discipline of meditation.

This is what I mean when I say that wisdom is both

one of the four directions of our practice and their goal. Over time and with discipline, we learn to anchor ourselves in the eye of the storm, and we learn, as Elijah did, that God is not in the storm or the earthquake or the fire, but in the still voice that calls us to the truth of who we are from the centre of our being. We learn that the present moment is the place where this calling is to be enacted by dwelling in the mindful awareness of God and learning to discern the wise choice as each decision moment of our lives becomes present and we choose the path of compassion.

We go from having experiences merely as events, evaluated by how they make us feel, to having experiences as moments of encounter with the deepest part of ourselves and with Divine Love, and so real wisdom arises and real discernment and transformation becomes possible.

When we live in this way, we are moving to a very deep way of being. We are choosing the way of transcendent wisdom. We seek it first by training ourselves in mindful awareness and then we deepen this choice by learning to meditate past the storms of our lives. But if we would go further and transcend the storms themselves, we can take the way of Elijah and let our meditative practice bring us to the mountain of God where, without our attention to feed them, the storms will blow themselves out.

There, anchored in meditative stillness through the breath and the word, we will realise that the storms are nothing to be afraid of. Rather they are opportunities to come to know at ever deeper levels the truth of our being as beloved always and as a place of Divine revelation. And even if they rage around us or within us, we know that by resting in the Divine Presence and by anchoring ourselves there with the breath and the word, we are like the disciples of Jesus who, when frightened of being overcome by the wild storms on the Sea of Galilee, called on Him for help and heard Him say to the storm, 'Quiet now! Be calm.' And we, like them before us, will say with astonishment as we see the calm waters of our now-still soul, 'Who can this be? Even the wind and the sea obey Him' (Mark 4:35–41). When we live in this way, we are living each moment as a door to wisdom; we arrive at inner equanimity and the storms are calmed.

Practice: A Wisdom Practice

Let us sit one more time.

Find a comfortable seat in a quiet space, place your feet flat on the floor and your back comfortably straight, take a moment to settle yourself and simply pause.

Just feel your feet upon the floor, your back against the chair.

Your mind is full of information, noise.

Things you want to grasp or hold on to, things you

are perhaps struggling with or maybe other issues, or ideas, or things that are waiting for you outside this room.

But, just for the moment, for this precious moment, come back to your breath, come back to that gentle rhythm of life within you, remembering that each in-breath and out-breath is a divine yes to you, to you existing, being, living.

Breathing in, we are aware of God.

Breathing out, we breathe out that love, that peace, that blessing to all.

Breathing in, I breathe in joy.

Breathing out, I breathe out peace.

Notice any points of tension within your body. Just gently allow your body to relax, loosen your jaw and neck, your shoulders and spine, anywhere there's tension, just try and release.

Don't struggle with it, just breathe into it, breathing in peace, breathing out love, following the circle of your breath, following it to the precious sacred point where the in-breath becomes the out-breath and the out-breath becomes the in-breath, resting in the light of God, the presence of God at the centre of your being, resting in the love of God, resting in the precious present moment.

As often as distractions come, we return to your breath – breathing in love, breathing out peace.

This is our practice; this is the place where He calms the storms of our lives and where we discover that with our minds and hearts in gentle attentiveness to God, even in the midst of the storm He is our peace.

And so we may like to give thanks in the following or other words:

'Glory to the Father
and to the Son
and to the Holy Spirit
as it was in the
beginning is now
and will be forever.
Amen.'

Come back now to the awareness of your breath.

Resting in your breath.

Breathing in peace.

Breathing out love.

Breathing in joy.

Breathing out calm.

Resting in your breath for three cycles of in-breath and out-breath.

Then gently begin to be aware of the chair supporting you, of your feet against the floor.

Take a moment to resolve to bring this peace into the rest of your day.

Practice: Basic Christian Meditation

If you want to begin this changed way of life and to pursue the four directions through a lens of explicit faith, through basic Christian meditation, what should you do? Well, the steps are very simple.

Find a comfortable seat in a quiet space, place your feet flat on the floor and your back comfortably straight, take a moment to settle yourself and simply pause.

You should not be rigid in any way.

You are not at war with your body.

You are relaxed and attentive, aware.

To begin with we make a deliberate act of intention, such as: 'Here I am, Lord.'

Begin to say the prayer word you have chosen with the rhythm of your own breath.

Don't change the rhythm of your breath.

Just let the prayer word rest within your breath.

This takes a little while but, eventually, you'll find a rhythm.

This is the hard bit, but it truly is transformative: listen to the word and do not deliberately think or imagine anything.

Yes, we know the distractions will come.

When they do, we greet them, smile at them and return to the breath and the word.

We end with an act of thanksgiving.

We do this, regularly, if possible daily, slowly building up to a practice of, ideally, twenty minutes twice a day.

Remember, there is nothing magical about the practice, nothing extraordinary: it's just the discipline of repetition that, over time, makes us more open to awareness of the presence of God.

As one of the old monks said, 'It is dropping water on a stone, drop by drop every day, until eventually the stone is dissolved.' We don't notice the stone dissolving; it's just that, one day, we suddenly realise it has dissolved. Or to go back to one of the early desert stories, one day the sun rises!

The beginner should not immediately go long at the start of the practice, because that may make you regret beginning at all. Two to three minutes, four or five times a day, is better than twenty-five minutes of agony in yourself.

If we want to deepen our meditation practice further we may then bring the 'Jesus Prayer' into our practice. This prayer practice is very ancient in the desert monastic tradition and comes directly from the meditative reading of the gospels wherein Jesus tells the story of the tax collector and the Pharisee (Lk 18: 9–14).

The Pharisee stands where all can see him in the temple and his 'prayer' is simply a list of egoic accomplishments and negative judgements of others. Meanwhile, the tax collector stands at the back of the temple, beats his breast and says, 'Lord have mercy on me, a sinner.'

Jesus says that it is the latter man who goes away in right relationship, in 'Shalom' with God, because the tax collector, sinner though he was, brought his truth to God and asked for mercy, while condemning no one else.

So, when we bring our truth into meditative awareness through the practice of the Jesus Prayer, we are saying to God, 'Lord, I know I cannot do this by myself. I need you in your mercy and compassion to accomplish this transformation in me.' And He will.

This is why this form of prayer became known as the prayer that 'pierces the heart' with the divine light of mercy and love, and opens us up to the needs of others, all while leading to perfect contemplative transformation. It accomplishes this because it brings the thinking mind down into the heart of ourselves where God dwells, through the breath and the repetition with awareness of the Divine Name of Christ.

If you want a very nice guide and a beautiful way of beginning to learn about the Jesus Prayer, I would heartily recommend the classic work called *The Way of a Pilgrim* and its sequel, *The Pilgrim Continues His Way*, of which there are many translations into English. It is written as a story of an anonymous pilgrim who travelled in the nineteenth century from teacher to teacher, asking about how we learn to pray the prayer, and is full of deep insight and good advice.

For now, though, let's look at a simple way of beginning to combine this prayer with our meditation practice.

Practice: Practising the Jesus Prayer

Find a comfortable seat in a quiet space, place your feet flat on the floor and your back comfortably straight, take a moment to settle yourself and simply pause.

The Jesus Prayer is one of the most ancient and one of the most powerful forms of meditative practice in the Christian tradition and is renowned for its transformative ability. In invoking the name of Jesus, we who are Christian believe we are invoking God, there and then, from whom the present moment is arising. Jesus is with us always, 'Behold I am with you until the end of the days' (Mt 28:20).

He is with us in every moment of prayer, and when we name Him and invoke His name, we're invoking the whole of who Jesus is – the salvation of God, the healing of God, the redemption of God, the love of God made visible and the One who is the Eternal Word and Wisdom through which all that is arises.

The Jesus Prayer originally, in its longest form, was: 'Lord Jesus Christ, son of the Living God, have mercy on me a sinner.' It was prayed either in two or four kinds of bursts, often matched to your in-breath and out-breath.

The Jesus Prayer

Lord Jesus Christ (breathing in)
Son of the Living God (breathing out)
Have mercy on me (breathing in)
A sinner (breathing out).

Over time, then, the practitioner breaks it down into two small pieces:

Lord Jesus Christ, son of the Living God
    (breathing in)
Have mercy on me a sinner (breathing out)

As the years go by it may even get shorter and smaller:

Lord Jesus Christ, have mercy.

Until, finally, it just finishes with the person repeating the name 'Jesus' as their prayer word, because the whole of the gospel as well as the whole of the prayer is contained within that most holy name.

To this day, this method is the essential meditative practice of Eastern Christian monasticism. Though it looks surprisingly simple, it is profoundly deep and immensely powerful when used as the heart of our meditative practice.

Christian Meditation:
Living the Love of the Holy Trinity

I remember once hearing the great Fr Laurence Freeman, a Benedictine abbot who writes extensively on Christian meditation, saying that, in this form of prayer, we are slowly moving from the idea of 'my prayer' (as being a list of what I want) to the 'prayer of the Trinity', which is simply beginning to participate in the inner life of God as an eternal communion of love that, in time, manifests in the prayer of Jesus in the garden, when He prays both as the Eternal Logos (or Second Person of the Trinity) and as the suffering servant of humanity: 'Not my will but your will be done.'

Padre Pio, one of our great Capuchin mystics, used to say the thing that people get wrong about prayer is thinking that God says no to our prayers. In Pio's view, God never says no to anything we ask. To him, there are only three answers God gives to prayer – yes; yes, but not now; and, finally, 'I have something even better in mind that will fulfil the very need you are bringing me but to a better degree.'

That is the communion of love we're dwelling in. Our meditative prayer seeks to establish that communion in a moment-to-moment basis. It gives us an extraordinary ability to enter into a new beginning. This form of meditation gives us the freedom and the blessing to constantly begin again in each moment, to recognise that creation has been held in existence in each moment by love, and that, with every breath we breathe out, God has to say yes to our existence in a loving way for us to be able to breathe in again!

God is saying yes constantly to you with each breath. This realisation is the perennial calming of the storms of our life.

A good way of looking at the relationship between meditation and mindfulness is what I call the 'way of the bowls'. This came to me in a shop many years ago when I was staring at a stack of bowls that went from bigger to smaller. I noticed that if I was on the same level as the largest bowl then I could not see the other smaller ones nested inside. But if I stood up and looked down, then all of the concentric rings of the bowls from the smallest at the centre to the circumference of the largest were visible. This set me thinking!

In the first steps of our Christian tradition, the cultivation of mindful awareness teaches us who we are in God in this moment and in our habitual patterns of being. We begin to see the large bowl. The basic conditions of our existence become visible. Over time, the practice of deeper meditation teaches us what we may become in God through a deepened awareness of His presence in each succeeding moment, and at deeper and deeper levels. We are beginning to stand up and look down and see the nesting bowls inside. That, in turn, leads to a discernment of God's will, guided by the two great gifts of scripture and tradition, and so the surrendering of negative patterns to grace begins. Now the bowls are being cleaned as well and we discover at the heart of the smallest bowl the presence of God.

This is the moment when we have created the conditions for contemplation to occur and the experience of the presence of God begins to effect the change in us to what we may become in God, and so we are cleared of all the useless detritus we have picked up along the way: we simply become an empty bowl to be filled with grace.

We have become still and we know – and the knowing is that which the psalmist talks about, not an intellectual knowing but, as the grannies used to say, a knowing in the blood and in the bone, a knowing in our very essence. This is the knowing that we are called to through stillness and silence. The knowing of God's presence in our very being as love, and it leads us also to an awareness of God's presence in everybody else too.

This doesn't lead us into an egoic 'I'm filled with God and therefore you are not'. It leads us to an awareness that we are all with God. So, eventually, our Christian mindfulness, through the cultivation of intentionality and the practice of inner attention, leads us into understanding how we must relate to ourselves and to all other creatures, from wisdom and with compassion.

Practice: Leaning Back into the Wisdom of the Four Directions of Meditation

Find a comfortable seat in a quiet space, place your feet flat on the floor and your back comfortably straight, take a moment to settle yourself and simply pause.

The contemplative stands still and breathes in the present moment at the junction of two axes and sees four inner directions revealed.

The two sacred axes are Meaning and Purpose.

The Four Inner Directions are:

Intention.

Attention.

Compassion.

Wisdom.

When purpose is joined with meaning, it becomes service.

When meaning is joined with purpose, it becomes transformation.

When attention is joined to intention, every moment becomes filled with meaning.

When intention is joined to attention, all of life becomes filled with purpose.

When attention is joined to the breath, the breath invites mindful awareness.

When intention is joined to the breath, then the breath becomes prayer.

For the fullness of prayer, let attention and intention be joined in the awareness of the breath as the place where we encounter Divine in-breathing.

For the fullness of life, let meaning and purpose be joined in the awareness of the present moment as the place of Divine Encounter and wisdom will arise.

When meaning and purpose are lived in each moment with attention and intention, we become aware that God is present in this moment and we are changed, transformed in the fire of His love into His likeness, sharing that love as compassion with all beings.

For us then, in each moment, anchored in the stillness and stability of our breathing . . .

Our intention is to become like Christ in each moment.

Our attention is on Christ in each moment.

Our purpose is to work with Christ in each moment.

Our meaning is in Christ in each moment and in eternity; for Christ is God, and God *is* Love . . .

We are still and we know.

We choose to dwell with awareness in the moment.

And the storms become calm.

Appendix 1

Meditation, Contemplation and the Holy Eucharist

The Eucharist and Meditative Prayer

From the very beginning of the Church, the path of meditation leading to contemplative prayer and the celebration of the Eucharist have been intimately connected – the one inviting a deeper participation in the other as the Catechism of the Catholic Church teaches:

'Entering into meditative prayer is like entering into the Eucharistic liturgy: we "gather up" the heart, recollect our whole being under the prompting of the Holy Spirit, abide in the dwelling place of the Lord which we are, awaken our faith in order to enter into the presence of him who awaits us. We let our masks fall and turn our hearts back to the Lord who loves us, so as to hand ourselves over to him as an offering to be purified and transformed.'

This beautiful paragraph builds marvellously on what we have just said. In a way, our participation in the Eucharist invites us again and again to trace the contemplative path, and our taking a meditative stance when celebrating the Eucharist enables us to deepen our levels of understanding of and participation in this great mystery.

St Bonaventure in his *Sermon on the Most Holy Body of Christ* reaffirms the importance of having this contemplative understanding of the Eucharist enabled so that we can participate as fully as possible in this great mystery of love:

'Whoever draws worthily near to the Eucharist obtains a quadruple grace. This sacrament instils the strength to operate; raises one to contemplation; disposes one towards knowledge of divine reality; animates and ignites contempt for the world and the desire for heavenly and eternal things, as it was said of Elijah who, with the force of that food walked up to the mountain of God, saw divine secrets and stopped at the entrance to the cave.'

According to Bonaventure, the Eucharist becomes our 'contemplative viaticum' (bread for the journey), which strengthens us, while also deepening our gifts of prayer and contemplation. There is simply no escaping the reciprocal relationship of contemplation and the Eucharist for the fathers, mothers, saints and mystics of the Church.

So, what happens to us when we take a contemplative

stance and begin the path of meditative prayer? How will it affect our participation in the Eucharist?

Well, one of the first things it does is to invite us to see deeply the mystery that we celebrate. We begin to understand that what we are present at is the representation of the supreme moment of human history.

There is an old proverb that you will still hear in Italy from time to time: 'At the table no one grows old.' It was co-opted some years ago into a marketing campaign for one of those olive-oil-butter-substitute spreads. In the television advertisement, we see a beautiful Mediterranean family busily spreading branded olive oil over their bread as the dulcet tones of the announcer claim that at this table no one grows old . . . presumably because of the youth-preserving qualities of olive oil!

However, what many of us probably don't know is that the marketing people got it wrong! The table referred to in the old proverb is the table of the Eucharist, the Altar. And the claim that at this table no one grows old was based on the faith of the early Christians that the celebration of the mass was a moment when we step into the eternal now of God's presence so fully that we are no longer governed by time. We are literally outside of time as *chronos* while celebrating the Eucharist.

Now I'm sure you, like me, have been bored so often at some masses as the preacher drones on that you have looked at your watch frequently and felt that no time was passing at all! But this isn't what is meant here.

Rather there is the understanding that, in some mysterious way, we are participating in an eternal moment: a nodal point of history where the eternal now of God intersects human history in the crucifixion of Christ. Jesus being fully God and fully human is the centre of this nodal point. Indeed, it would be better to say that He is the centre point of all history, in that our story finds its origins, its ongoing existence and its fulfilment in Him.

This means that our prayer life, our desire to have relationship with God and to communicate with Him on ever deeper levels of love – what we call the contemplative or meditative path in Christianity – must always relate to and be centred upon the person of Jesus.

And if we centre our prayer life and meditation practice on Jesus, as the one who reveals the Father's face, then we will also centre our life on the table where no one grows old, on the mass. For this is the place in time where we come face to face with the ultimate eternal act of Divine Compassion, the sacrifice of Jesus as the Lamb of God who takes away the sins of the world.

The fathers saw this as the moment when the old pagan understanding of time as the destroyer, *chronos*, that eats up our lives by the minute is conquered by the intersection of the eternal dimension, the *kairos* of Christ. The time of the new and perpetual jubilee arrives with the incarnation of Jesus and His announcing of the Kingdom, and it remains forever open to us through His death and resurrection.

We encounter these salvific moments that are at once historical and eternal in every celebration of the mass. However, often we are too busy or distracted to be present to these extraordinary events.

Perhaps as a Church we have spent so long talking about the Real Presence of Jesus in the Eucharist that we have forgotten that we must also work on our side to be really present to Him!

Fostering a Eucharistic Meditative Stance

The contemplative Christian seeks to live always in the awareness of this eternal dimension, this interpenetration of time and eternity. We live in incarnational awareness with the understanding that all of creation has been rendered holy again by the entry of Jesus into our world.

So, in building contemplative moments into our days, moments of prayerful pausing that enable us to come face to face with this mystery or, as St Clare puts it in her third letter to St Agnes of Prague, 'to place our minds before the mirror of eternity', we create a chain of experience that enables us to begin to live in the presence of the Lord here and now, to be really present to the One who is always present to us.

Practices that help with this are as old as Christianity: Lectio Divina, the praying of the Psalms, the Jesus Prayer, the Rosary, the Divine Office, Centring Prayer, Practice of the Presence of God, the Sacrament of the Present Moment – all of these methods and many others have at their core the goal of uniting the person with the presence of God who is present to them.

They enable us to journey, like Elijah, into the cave of the heart, there to wait, to abide in stillness until the storms of emotions, stresses and thoughts have abated, and we are calm enough to discern the voice of God within.

The mass is, of course, at a completely different level of 'practice', but our participation in it may be deepened by applying to it some of the techniques that come from the prayer practices that we have mentioned above. Bringing times of stillness and quiet into our celebration of the sacred liturgy is the most important.

These times give us a moment or two for the words of the liturgy and the scriptures of the day to anchor themselves in our minds, so that we may have fuel for our prayerful pauses later that day. After all, how often have you left a celebration of mass unable to remember the readings that you have just heard? It happens to me so often!

Following on from silence and stillness, the next most important practice to bring to our celebration of the mass is that of posture. We forget at times that we are embodied! We are psycho-biological entities that have a sacramental world view: in other words, our bodies, and what they are doing, are just as important to how we pray as are our thoughts and feelings.

Indeed, our thoughts and feelings will often be much better and more deeply centred if our posture is appropriate to what we are saying or thinking. Yes, there is a body-language of prayer, commented on by the monastics of the Church from the days of the Desert Fathers onwards. Moving from standing to sitting to kneeling to bowing to prostrating reminds us of the truths that we are celebrating and takes us out of a 'spectator mentality' so often present in today's liturgy. Where the body goes the mind and heart will follow.

Arising from our encounter with this eternal salvific moment in the mass we are, in turn, driven to deepen our prayer life so that we become ever more aware of our need to be healed, to make this transformative journey into *theosis*, the transformation of the human being through the power of the Holy Spirit into an ever more accurate image of Christ.

We become aware of our own soul-sickness, our sinfulness, though without anxiety or fear; and, at the same time, we see that the perfect remedy for that sickness has been provided in the Holy Eucharist. It is no wonder, then, that one of the earliest images by which the Church described itself was as the 'field hospital of humanity' – the place where those who know they are sick come in order to be healed.

It is interesting to note that the saints assure us that the self-knowledge that arises through prayer would be too much for us if we didn't know that God has already provided the means by which we may be healed. To the earliest monks and nuns, daily communion was encouraged as an inoculation against sin. As St Ambrose wrote in *'On the Mysteries' and the Treatise on the Sacraments*: 'Anyone who is wounded looks for healing. For us, it is a wound to be liable to sin. Our healing lies in the adorable heavenly Sacrament.'

St Thérèse of Lisieux writes in her letters that nothing should prevent us from receiving the Lord, not even our sin. In one famous letter, she teaches that when we have repented in heart and have the resolution to go to confession as soon as is possible, we should be confident of the Lord's mercy and go to receive the medicine that He has provided for our ultimate healing, a place of communion here and now in the sacred present moment that touches eternity and is healed by this sacrament of Divine Love.

Poetry Pause

Emmaus Fire

We forget the onceness of it all,
His isness the ever-present
Presence joining them
And us along the way of grief.
The dry tinder of their walking hearts,
Long drained of ease of tears
Seeking the relief of action and escape
Become a conflagration now of single word spark
made
The hidden One who walked with them
Who broke their bread to mend their hearts
Was even then appearing to women, apostles,
poor lost Peter
Resurrection broke not just the tomb but time
itself
Unleashed eternity upon an unsuspecting world
His wounds the unwinding backwards
Of the tight twine of history's binding
While resurrection power handfasts
Us all the more to blessedness
All while assuring futures of us yet unborn and
unthought-of by all but Him,
Seeing us and seeing them and all who were and
would be

In one simple moment of love, in one always open
eye
Lamb and Ram and Scapegoat all at once He is
We tell our tales of this and this and this
Our Gospels bound by time and place our stories
Reach from once upon to ever after with quest
between
Yet all that happened on that morn was then
at once, and ever after both
Flamed and fired and formed anew our history
In the cracked kiln of His heart
And that is really now, and here,
So come now upon this dusty road
Where deep looking you will see
Flaming footprints at your side
A burning in your heart
as the bread of moments breaks
in holed and holy hands
As you Emmaus walk with me

Appendix 2

Bibliography

Christian Meditation and Contemplation Classics

Anonymous, *The Book of Privy Counsel*, Paraclete Press, 2015.

Anonymous, *The Cloud of Unknowing*, Paraclete Press, 2015.

Anonymous, *The Pilgrim Continues His Way*, Random House Publishing, 1985.

Anonymous, *The Way of a Pilgrim*, Random House Publishing, 1985.

Brother Lawrence of the Resurrection, *The Practice of the Presence of God*, Martino Fine Books, 2016.

Catechism of the Catholic Church, Image, 2003.

d'Ávila, St Teresa, *The Way of Perfection*, ICS Publications, 2000.

de Caussade, Fr Jean Paul, *Abandonment to Divine Providence*, 2010.

Evagrius Ponticus, *The Praktikos*, Oxford University Press, 2003.

St Ambrose, *'On the Mysteries' and the Treatise On the Sacraments*, Isha Books, 2013.

St Augustine, *The Confessions*, Penguin Classics, 2003.

St Bonaventure, *Sermon on the Most Holy Body of Christ*, Franciscan Publications, St. Bonaventure University Press.

St Catherine of Siena, *The Dialogue*, Tan Books, 1991.

St Clare, *The Third Letter of St Clare to St Agnes of Prague, Francis and Clare: The Complete Works*, Paulist Press, 1986.

St Francis de Sales, *Introduction to the Devout Life*, SPCK Publishing, 2017.

St John Vianney, *The Little Catechism of the Cure of Ars*, Tan Books, 2014.

St Thérèse of Lisieux, *The Story of a Soul*, Tan Books, 2015.

The Sayings of the Desert Fathers, Trans. Sr. Benedicta Ward, Penguin, 2003.

Talbot, John Michael, *The Admonitions of St Francis of Assisi*, San Damiano Books, 2019.

The Philokalia, Trans. Kalistos Ware, Faber and Faber, 1983.

Modern Spirituality

Bourgeault, Cynthia, *The Wisdom Jesus*, Shambala, 2008.

Chesterton, G.K., *The Defendant*, Dover Publications Inc., 2012.

Clement, Olivier, *The Roots of Christian Mysticism*, New City Publishing, 2015.

Davidson, Richard J and Lutz, Antoine, 'Buddha's Brain: Neuroplasticity and Meditation', *Signal Process Mag.*, 25(1): 176–174, 2008.

DeMello SJ, Anthony, *Awareness*, Collins, 1990.

Georgiou, Steve, *The Way of the Dreamcatcher: Spirit Lessons with Robert Lax*, Editions Novalis, 2002.

Hendrick, Br Richard, *Still Points*, Hachette Books Ireland, 2022.

Johnston SJ, Fr William, *Mystical Theology*, Harper Collins, 1995.

Johnston SJ, Fr William, *Silent Music*, Fordham University Press, 1997.

Kabat-Zinn, Jon, *Full Catastrophe Living, Revised Edition: How to Cope with Stress, Pain and Illness Using Mindfulness Meditation*, Piatkus, 2013.

Kasimov, Harold (ed.), *Beside Still Waters: Jews, Christians, and the Way of the Buddha*, Wisdom Publications US, 2003.

Keating OCSO, Abbot Thomas, *Open Mind, Open Heart*, Bloomsbury, 2003.

Kornfield, Jack, *After the Ecstasy, the Laundry*, Rider Press, 2000.

Laird OSA, Fr Martin, *Into the Silent Land*, Darton, Longman and Todd, 2006.

Main OSB, Dom John, *Word into Silence*, Canterbury Press, 2006.

Markides, Kyriacos, *The Mountain of Silence*, Image Books, 2002.

Markides, Kyriacos, *Gifts of the Desert*, Doubleday Books, 2006.

Mathewes-Green, Frederica, *Praying the Jesus Prayer*, Paraclete Press, 2011.

Merton, Thomas, *Love and Living*, Farrar, Strauss and Giroux, 1979.

Merton, Thomas, *Seeds of Contemplation*, Anthony Clarke Books, 1972.

Needleman, Jacob, *Lost Christianity*, Element Books, 1990.

Nouwen, Henri, *Desert Wisdom: Sayings of the Desert Fathers*, Orbis Books USA, 2002.

New Revised Standard Version Updated Edition, National Council of Churches of Christ in the United States of America, 2021.

Snowden, Dr David, *Aging with Grace*, Fourth Estate, 2011.

The Carthusian Novice Conferences Book Series, Darton, Longman and Todd, 1995.

Van de Weyr, Robert, *Celtic Fire*, Darton, Longman and Todd, 1990.

Williams, Mark and Penman, Danny, *Mindfulness: Finding Peace in a Frantic World*, Piatkus, 2011.

Acknowledgements

A book like this is always a cumulative effort. In its pages, I have done my best to introduce the meditative tradition to a new audience in a way that speaks to many people. However, the wisdom present within these pages comes from the many teachers and masters I have met along the way. Where I have failed to pass on their wisdom, well, the error is mine and not theirs!

To my teachers, both living in this world and in the next, I offer my deepest and most profound thanks for sharing your wisdom with me. Foremost amongst these are my Capuchin brothers, who never fail to inspire me and to challenge me to live a life of greater fidelity each day. I am unworthy to be numbered among them and I thank them all for their patience, kindness and forgiveness, not to mention the wisdom they live and the inspiration I get from so many of them who are so much more faithful to the practice of all I have attempted to share here than I am.

To my family, once again, I offer heartfelt thanks for your patience with me, for your kindness and for your love. I would be lost without you all. You are home, and that says it all.

To all at the Sanctuary who, over the years, have invited me to become a teacher there while you have all taught me instead. Special thanks to Sister Stan and Sister Sheila, to Niamh and Jane, to Tony and John, to Mark and James and to all who have made it and continue to make it such a special place.

To all at Hachette Books Ireland, especially Ciara and Elaine. I offer my sincere gratitude for their unending belief in this book and their even greater patience with me over the past year as it was slowly written.

Finally, as always, I offer my deepest bow of thanks to the Lady of the Angels, the Seat of Wisdom and Queen of the Franciscan Order to whom I dedicate this and all my work. Please keep me and all who come to read this little book, and all involved in its making, safe from all storms beneath your mantle of peace.

Brother Richard

In an uncertain world, we all seek a sense of security and inner peace. *Still Points: A Guide to Living the Mindful Meditative Way* shows us how to achieve this, simply by following a daily spiritual practice. In doing so, we enter into a deep connection to sacred stillness, revealing to us the beauty within the present moment.

In a book that can be followed throughout the year, or dipped in and out of to find 'still points' in times of distraction and worry, Brother Richard brings us on a transformative journey of meditation, poetry and sacred pause, enabling us to experience a sense of peace, happiness and belonging in our lives.

'*Still Points* is a call to stop, to consider, to see the beauty and sacredness of ourselves in everyone and everything' SISTER STAN